THE WAY

BIBLE STUDY SERIES
& DAILY DEVOTIONAL

Scripture quotations are taken from King James, New King James, New International and the Living Bible Versions of the Bible, unless otherwise indicated.

THE WAY
Bible Study Series & Daily Devotional V
ISBN: 0-9727614-5-4

Produced in the United States of America by *Nestto Graphix*

For Copies and more information, contact:

C.A.C. WOSEM
108-02 Sutphin Blvd. Jamaica, NY 11435
Tel: (718) 658-8981 Fax: (718) 658-5317
www.christapostlolicchurch.org

Acknowledgment

The effort of everybody that put in their time into the production of this year's Bible Study Series is highly commendable.

Editors
Oluwatoyosi Dairo, Abraham Obadare
Olufunmilola Awosiyan, Florence Oluwasanmi
Justus Orori, Christopher Adebayo, Nike Adesiyakan
Queens, NY. Assembly Bible Students

Contributors
Oluwatoyosi Dairo, Esther Obadare,
Deborah Famuyide, Ayodele Olulana, Abraham Obadare
Costain Phiri, Temitope Ademuwagun, Patrick Abohwo
Florence Oluwasanmi, Ayokunle Fatukasi.

Page Layout & Word Processing
Julie Akinola, Abraham Obadare, Olubunmi Dairo

Cover Design
Henry Ayensu

HOW TO USE THIS SUNDAY SCHOOL BOOKLET

The topics addressed in this booklet are intended to give a practical approach to the various teachings of the Bible. Contents are divided on a monthly basis as a guide. At the beginning of each month, the teacher should go over the studies for the month and plan how to spread the teaching to cover the allotted time in your local assembly, fellowship or household. It is recommended that all Sunday School Teachers undertake a review prior to the teaching. This will enhance knowledge sharing among the teachers.

It is advisable not to rush teachings in order to allow meaningful assimilation of issues discussed in the study.

Studies generally follow this pattern:

Topic
Text: Brief passage(s) relating to the topic to be addressed.
Memory Verse: Single verse which members are supposed to memorize.
Focus: Lessons to be learnt by the end of the study.
Introduction: Brief overview of the discussion.
Main body of the discussion:
Numbered or divided into sub-heads.
Questions: For interactive discussion or thought provocation.
Conclusion: Take home message.
Prayer(s): For God's help to do what is taught.
Daily Bible Reading: Meant for weekly devotionals to further widen the scope of knowledge on the subject matter. It also draws comparison with other related topics.

Deaconess (Dr.) Oluwatoyosi Dairo
Sunday School Superintendent

TABLE OF CONTENTS

Month	Lesson	Title	Page

1

VESSELS IN THE HOUSE
Text: 2 Tim. 2:19-22

Memory Verse:

"But in a great house there are not only vessels of gold and silver, but also of wood and clay, some for honor and some for dishonor"
(2 Tim. 2:20, NKJV).

Focus:

The focal point of this study is to affirm that a "vessel" is anyone God can use.

Introduction:

The church (ecclesia), the assembly or congregation is the great house. The individual believer is the vessel. A vessel of honor is anyone that uses the treasures God has deposited in them. He or she utilizes the treasure to do the work of the kingdom; to serve. A Vessel is a utensil, container or receptacle. A believer is a container. There is spiritual treasure that God has deposited in us. We are earthen vessels but we carry spiritual treasures and gifts. What brings honor is what we make of these treasures. When we, the utensils, employ the gifts to build the kingdom we are bringing honor unto God and setting ourselves up for rewards.

Class Participation

1. How do I discover who I am?

2. What if my church has no ministry for clay? Do I become gold, silver or wood? You need to understand that our individuality is our strength.

7

What does the Bible teach?

To discover who I am, I must know what gifts I have been given. Rom 12:4-8 says, *"For as we have many members in one body, but all the members do not have the same function, so we, being many, are one body in Christ, and individually members of one another. Having then gifts differing according to the grace that is given to us, let us use them: if prophecy, let us prophesy in proportion to our faith; or ministry, let us use it in our ministering; he who teaches, in teaching; he who exhorts, in exhortation; he who gives, with liberality; he who leads, with diligence; he who shows mercy, with cheerfulness"* (NKJV).

Our gifts differ. All of us have received the grace to work in the house of God according to these individual gifts. Clay has the gift of building; gold has the gift of shining. Clay should not fight gold over who shines most because it has already found greatness in building. Gold should not fight the wood in the building department. There is enough ministry in shining. We need to know that the body of Christ is joined and knitted together by what every joint supplies, according to the effective working by which every part does its share, causing the body to grow to the edifying of itself in love. (Eph. 4:16) This is informing me that I need to identify my gift and build on it, stay in it, grow in it, and edify the church with it.

If my church has no ministry to feed my gift, that does not mean I am excluded. If the word of God says each individual has his/her part to play but my church is yet to put my part in place, all I need do is to start that ministry in my church with appropriate permission. You could start a prison ministry if there is none in your church. If you have a gift of mercy, show mercy whole heartedly by starting a ministry for widows, the homeless, etc.

Conclusion

Every vessel in a great house has its own usefulness. Differences in application do not translate to redundancy of any vessel.

The Lord is expecting you to know that you are vessel in His hands and to find out how you can be your best and glorify God. Without a life surrendered to Jesus Christ our services will not be meaningful.

Prayer

Father help me to live a life of usefulness in thy sight.

Daily Bible Reading

1. It is only good trees that bear good fruits (Mt 7:16-20).
2. The position of a honorable vessel must not be traded for anything else (Heb. 12:15-17).
3. Vessels unto Honor must be useful and active wherever they find themselves (Acts 8:4-8).
4. Vessels unto Honor cooperate with God to renew them for His purpose (1 Tim. 1: 12-17)
5. Vessels of honor cannot work without the help of the Holy Spirit (1 Cor. 12: 1-11).
6. We need one another for full actualization of our potentials (1 Cor. 12: 12-27).

Knowledge enhancement Resource:
Read day 17 of "Purpose driven life" – by Rick Warren

VESSELS UNTO HONOR
Text: 2 Timothy 2:19-21

Memory Verse:
But we have this treasure in earthen vessels, that the excellence of the power may be of God and not of us.
2 Cor. 4:7 NKJV

Focus
To examine my readiness for God's use.

Introduction:
Vessels unto honor are endlessly useful vessels. 2 Tim 2:20-21 says, *"But in a great house there are not only vessels of gold and silver, but also of wood and clay, some for honor and some for dishonor. Therefore if anyone cleanses himself from the latter, he will be a vessel for honor, sanctified and useful for the Master, prepared for every good work"* (NKJV). The one million dollar question is, "am I useful?" Not "am I gold, silver, wood or clay." If wood is carrying the tabernacle, it is useful wood. If clay builds our walls, it is useful, and so are gold and silver if they lend themselves to God's use. If I use my gold to carry corruption, it is unto dishonor just as much as any clay used for sin or corruption. Honor is a by-product of application and not composition.

Class Participation:
1. How do I become a vessel unto honor?
2. If I am suppose to serve God with honor, how do I make myself ready?
3. Isn't it just enough to be saved? Do I have to serve for honor?

What does the Bible teach?
The Bible teaches that we have all been called according to God's purpose (Rm. 8:28). If salvation means God has called me

to His Kingdom, then it is obvious that He has a purpose for me. So I must begin by finding my purpose. I cannot say that God cannot use me because there are so many people already doing something. If He has called me, my purpose must be unique.

To make myself ready all I need is the WORD. In 2 Tim. 2:15, the Bible says that I need to study to show myself approved, a worker who does not bring shame to God or to self. I must also live holy. The Bible says I must cleanse myself from the filthiness of flesh and the spirit, perfecting holiness in the fear of God. If a vessel is dirty, it cannot carry anything worthy. I am a carrier of God's glory.

Another step I need to constantly take is to depart from iniquity. *(2 Tim. 2:19) says, "Nevertheless the solid foundation of God stands, having this seal, the Lord knows those who are His and let everyone who names the name of Christ depart from iniquity"*

To know God is a good thing, to serve God is a great honor. We must seek excellence through service. We must please God by first of all living holy and also serving Him in kingdom building.

It is one thing for one to know God, and it is another thing for God to know one. We must all strive to be known by God, not just as anybody but as vessels unto honor. One whom the almighty God can use. We must live not as one who owns himself or herself but one owned by God (Gal. 2:20). God's name is attached to us and there is great demand on our character. When we serve Him and do good, it brings glory to Him (Matt. 5). God emphasizes the "doing." This is why James 1:22 says, be doers of the word and not hearers only, deceiving yourselves. Verse 25 emphasizes doing the work.

So vessels of honor walk in righteousness; pursuit of, faith, love, peace with those who call on the Lord out of a pure heart. They are gentle to all, able to teach, and patient with others.

What vessels of honor are:
- Vessels of honor are always ready for service, creative and purposeful.
- Vessels of honor are Holy Spirit-filled and word-empowered.
- Vessels of honor use their treasures.
- They think of what they can do for the Church, and not what the church can do for them.
- Vessels of honor are kingdom builders.
- Vessels of honor initiate more than they follow.
- Vessels of honor are satisfied with their Godly gifting and individuality.
- Vessels of honor possess vision.

What vessels of honor are not:
- They are not lustful
- They do not engage in foolish and ignorant disputes
- They do not generate strife, they generate activities
- They do not engage in quarrelling (Mk. 9:50)
- They do not curse (Rom. 12:4).
- They do not abuse (Col. 4:6)
- They do not backbite (Ps. 15:3)

Extra Reading:
Examples of Vessels unto honor (Women)
- Sarah (Gen. 21:1-2); Ruth (Ruth 1:16); Abigail (1 Sam. 25: 23-24); Elizabeth (Luke. 1:36-37); Priscilla (Roman 16:3-5); Deborah (Judges 4:4); Esther (Esther 4:16); Mary (John 2:5); Dorcas (Acts 9:36); Phoebe (Romans. 16:1)

Examples of Vessels unto Honor (Men)
- Moses (Ex. 4:18); Elijah & Elisha (2 Kings 1:10-14, 4:33-35); Daniel (Daniel 6:4-5); Shadrach, Meshach & Abednego (Daniel 3:12); Joshua (Joshua 1:1-2); Joseph (Gen. 45:4-5); Ezekiel (Ezek. 37:1).

Conclusion:

The material constitution notwithstanding, the refinement process a material has been subjected to will determine its eventual use. God is waiting to bless what He has deposited in you and make you a blessing to the whole world. Sharpen yourself to become the honorable utensil in the hands of God. There are so many souls to save, so many needs to meet and many people to encourage.

Prayer

Father, please help me to live for you as a vessel unto honor.

Daily Bible Reading

1. Vessels of honor have integrity (Prov. 22:1-2)
2. Without being tried, you cannot attain excellence (James 1: 1-15).
3. Whatever ability we exhibit, we received it from God, so there is should be no place for pride (James 1:16-20).
4. It takes practice of Gods word to purge ourselves of all impurity (James 1: 21-27).
5. Vessels of honor are people of character (Col. 3: 1-17).

6. Whatever you do, do with humility knowing others are gifted also (Romans 12:3-6).

Knowledge enhancement Resource
Read Dr. Frederick Price's book "Integrity"
Read Rick Warren's "Purpose Driven Life"

3

CARING FOR MINISTERS

Text: 1 Corinthians 9:1-12.

Memory Verse:

"Who ever goes to war at his own expense?
Who plants a vineyard and does not eat of the
fruit? Or who tends a flock and does not drink
of the milk of the flock?"
(1 Cor. 9:7, NKJV).

Focus:

- Understand the need for caring for the ministers of God
- Establish that ministers were cared for throughout different eras in the Bible.

Introduction

Caring for ministers is not a frequently addressed topic. Pastors do not often teach the subject, so they would not be seen as indirectly asking for gifts. The subject of giving to ministers was practiced before the dispensation of grace, and continued in the New Testament. Paul was very open about the issue, and his writings shed more light on this often-neglected subject. Ignorance about this subject is a subtle way of the enemy to hinder the blessings associated with such practices. As we begin a new year, we want every reader to tap into this special area of unlimited blessings from God. 1 Tim. 5:17-18 helps us to know that our ministers are spiritually employed and deserve their wages, benefits, bonuses, gifts, etc. from the flock.

Why should ministers be cared for?
1. They sow to the congregation spiritually, so in return they are to reap our material things (1 Cor. 9: 11). Just as we work and get paid and many at times have additional

benefits, ministers are to derive benefits from sowing into our lives spiritually, aside from getting a salary if any.

2. The Lord has commanded that those who preach the gospel should live from it (1 Cor. 9:14, Matt. 10:10).

3. So that they may devote their time to seek God instead of sustenance (2 Chro. 31:4)

Caring for the men of God makes them to be more dedicated to the spiritual work, making them more available for the spiritual responsibility that God has given to them. God wants us to demonstrate our affection to Him through love, support and care for Ministers He has delegated to shepherd His people.

Caring for priests in Moses' era (Num. 35:1-4).
- God instructed Moses to command the Israelites that they give the Levites cities to dwell in out of their (Israelites) inheritance. The Levites were also to have a common land for their cattle.

Practical Application
Relating this to the present day, ministers are entitled to an unquestionable regular income, but extras that are also needed should come from their congregation. Hence the instruction to share part of their inheritance with the priest was a command not an option. We can link this right to partake of the material wealth of the Christians to what Paul refers to in 1 Cor. 9:11-13. This right was however not abused
- The cities that were given to the Levites were in proportion to the inheritance each tribe received (Num. 35: 8). Hence what ministers benefit from individual members of the congregation should be proportional to their substance.

Caring for priests post Mosaic era
- God commanded the widow of Zarephath to provide for Elijah in the time of famine (1 Kings 17: 8-9). It implies that God does not intend His ministers to

suffer. Under no circumstance should ministers be deprived of what is needed for sustenance.

- Hezekiah commanded the people to give support to the priests and Levites (2 Chro. 31:4).
- Saul ensured they had something to give to the man of God as they went to enquire from him (1 Sam.9: 6-8). As Christians, we can learn from this example, show this gesture to ministers when their services are required to meet our needs. Such services to name a few include house warming, dedications, naming ceremonies, birthday parties etc. These gifts do not mean we are paying them for their services (you cannot pay for the anointing), but tokens of appreciation.

Caring For Ministers in Jesus' era.
Mary Magdalene, Joanna and other women ministered to Jesus (Luke 8:1-3). If Jesus required to be ministered to, then who does not?

Caring For Ministers Post Jesus era
Paul recorded that the care of the Philippians' church for him had flourished (Phil. 4:10). Paul was not a pauper by any standard. The church repeatedly took care of him irrespective of where he was. This was the basis of the popular prayer many love to quote, but forget to do what led to the prayer (Phil.4: 18).

Prayer
God grant me a deeper understanding of the benefits of caring for ministers.

Question
Can I use my tithe as a gift to a minister?

Conclusion
Sowing into your minister's life opens doors of blessing for you. The life of your minister is definitely a good soil into

which you should sow and of course expect good harvest. Reading Luke 6:38 helps us to know the amount of blessings you will receive in return. The care for ministers transcends all different eras in the scripture. While ministers are not looking onto individual members for sustenance, members should not forget to communicate in good things to those who have sown spiritual things into their lives. The privilege should not be abused as Paul categorically stated that they did not exercise their right on the church. Undue demands should not be placed on church membership.

Daily Bible Reading

1. The Apostles' provision was to be met on their missionary journey. They were not supposed to make additional provision by themselves (Matt. 10:5-14).
2. Paul did not covet anyone's possession (Acts 20: 32-36).
3. Onessiphorus took care of Paul even when many had deserted him (2 Tim. 1:15-18)
4. Mary Magdalene and other women had the privilege of hearing first about Christ's resurrection (Luke 24:1-12).
5. Nabal's refusal to provide for David and his men would have led to the destruction of his whole household, but for the wisdom of Abigail (1 Sam. 25:2-13).
6. Abigail took care of David and his men (1 Sam. 25:14-31).

MINISTERS' NEEDS

Text: Philippians 4: 10, 14-20

Memory Verse:

"Not that I seek the gift, but I seek the fruit that abounds to your account"
(Phil. 4: 17).

Focus:

- Know how to care for the ministers of God through case studies recorded in the Bible
- Highlight the reward of caring for ministers of God.

Introduction

As indicated by Apostle Paul, it is indeed expedient for Ministers of God to benefit from the fruitfulness of the congregation in as much they minister to their spiritual needs. The blessings of God abound to brethren because of their knowledge, understanding and obedience to the word of God taught by His ministers. Even in situations where we have not directly benefited from the ministrations of an Apostle, but because of our understanding of the spiritual role of the men of God, we should still provide for the needs of the men of God (the Shunamite woman).

PASTORS SHOULD RECEIVE:

Acceptance: It is one thing to have a pastor and it is another to accept that pastor as one's shepherd. Jesus clearly states that we need to receive and accept His servants who are placed over us.

- When you accept and honor your minister of God, you are accepting Jesus who sent him / her, and when you disrespect or disregard the anointing of God upon him or her, you reject Jesus (John 13:20).
- He who receives a prophet in the name of a prophet shall receive a prophet's reward. And he who receives a

righteous man in the name of a righteous man shall receive a righteous man's reward (Matt. 10:41-42 NKJV).

Many Christians reap no benefits from the anointing in the lives of their ministers because of failure to whole-heartedly accept them as ones sent to them by God. Jesus had a similar scenario among His own people who only thought of Him as carpenter's son. As such He could only do a few miracles there (Mark 6:1-6).

Obedience & Respect: When ministers are obeyed, it is easier for them to discharge their duties effectively. Each time the Israelites rebelled against Moses, it provoked God's anger, to the point that Moses himself lost his calm. All the rebellious ones died in the wilderness.
- Respect and be loyal to the minister of God (Luke 20:25).
- Avoid participating in libel against him or her (1 Tim. 5:19); and
- Do not grieve him / her by disrespecting or despising his / her spouse.
- Many people have touched the anointed and harmed the servant of God through idle talks, contrary to the instruction in Psalm 105:15.

We should also know that it is hypocrisy to respect a minister and despise his/her spouse. The minister is incomplete without his/her spouse. Do not maltreat the spouse of a minister and expect the best performance from him. It is wisdom to carry along the minister's spouse if your duty / work warrants closeness to the minister and you are of the opposite sex.

Prayer: Paul repeatedly coveted the prayers of the people. He requested prayers for the word to move forward as it should, for ability to speak the mysteries of Christ (Col. 4: 2-4). It is not only pastors that should pray for the congregation. For the best to come forth from ministers, the prayers of the saints go a long way. Pray for their health, family, protection and more anointing of God upon their lives (1 Tim. 2:1-2.).

Service & Support: Moses had to be in the presence of God with outstretched arms (held the rod in his hand) while Joshua fought Amalek. It got to a time that his hands became heavy. Amalek prevailed whenever his hands were lowered. Hur and Aaron had to support him, for victory to be won (Exo. 17: 9-13). Care given to Moses hands translated to victory for the entire nation. One wonders how many battles a whole congregation has lost, just because nobody perceived that the minister needed a little support to pull everyone through at a point in time. Also note that it is not every issue that needs the minister's attention. That is why both administrative and spiritual structures are set up in the church like Moses set up to settle matters (Exo. 18: 24-26). This frees up the minister to timely attend to other spiritual things (Exo. 18: 19).

Rewards of caring for men of God
- We please God through our sacrifice (Phil. 4:18).
- It causes a release of blessings into our lives (Phil. 4:18). The Shunamite's woman received the gift of a child from the word of Elisha simply because he was touched by the extreme care he received from her (2 Kings 4: 8-14).
- It supernaturally connects us to God's provision and sustenance even in difficult times (1 Kings 17: 13-14). The widow and her entire household had enough supplies in the time of famine, because she took care of Elijah.
- It provokes divine favor to intervene when required (2 Kings 8: 5-8).

Questions
1. What does respecting the spouse of a man of God have to do with the church?
2. Why do we need to pray for ministers since they are supposed to be more spiritual than members?

Conclusion:
Caring for and honoring your minister is the word of God and it is for your benefit (2 Chronicles 20:20), therefore, it must be done as an act of obedience to God.

Prayer

Father forgive us in every area that we might have neglected our ministers.

Daily Bible Reading

1. The widow had more than enough throughout famine (1 Kings 17:8-16).
2. The shunamite woman had first hand information about the on coming famine and how to escape it (2 Kings 8: 1-5).
3. Rahab supported the spies that were sent to Jericho when the inhabitants wanted to kill them (Joshua 2:1-21).
4. Mary anointed Jesus with costly oil (John 12: 1-7).
5. Be careful about passing judgments against the man of God (1 Tim. 5:19)
6. Abigail (now widow) became David's wife for her previous care for him (1 Sam. 25: 39-42). This does not imply that we should expect payback from ministers when we care for them.

5

REPUTABLE SOURCE BUT BAD COUNSEL

Text: 2 Sam. 17:1-4

Memory Verse
*"Therefore do not be unwise, but understand what
the will of the Lord is"*
(Eph. 5:17).

Focus
- To teach weighing all advices before acting on them.
- To encourage us to place God's will above any human advice.

Introduction
Advices from reputable sources should not be undermined. However, advices have to be weighed in the light of God's word before they are acted upon. The reputation of the source of an advice should therefore not be the sole consideration that informs our decisions.

Ahithophel to Absalom (2 Sam. 16:20-23).
Ahithophel was a respected counselor of David. His reputation in counseling was so great, that it was likened unto a man that inquired from the oracle of God. As such, Absalom did a wise thing by inquiring from such a reputable source. However the advice was contrary to the will of God. The implication of Absalom going into his father's concubines abhorred his father, thereby further estranging him from David. Moreover, God did not anoint him king. The advice was intended to help Absalom strengthen his claim to the throne, but in the end, he died a shameful death.

Practical Application
'Good' and reputable members in the church have wrongly led many simple Christians in rebelling against authority. Without searching the scriptures, they fall prey of bad advices. No matter how reputable the source of your advice, if it is not in keeping with the written word of God it should not be accepted.

The Old prophet and the man of God from Judah (1 Kings 13:11-24).
The man of God from Judah was most likely younger in the ministry than the old prophet. Hence, by experience the older man could hear 'better' from God than the younger. There was however no confusion about the instruction God gave the young man, because he had earlier turned down such an offer that was contrary to God's instruction (1 Kings 13:7-10). The reputation of the source of his advice probably made him give in contrary to God's will. Unfortunately, it was the same person that caused him to err, that God used to meet judgment on him.

Practical Application
As a child of God, you must be filled with the spirit of God and practice listening to God. Whenever you are convinced about what God has communicated to you do not be intimidated by another's spiritual status. Let the decision you make in your Christian journey not be based on someone else's conviction.

Sarai to Abram (Gen. 16:1-6).
The love between this couple was commendable. Sarai would rather have her husband be a father anyhow than wait for God's time. Coming from the woman of the house, making an offer for what you longed for why not? Abram felt it was okay since it

23

came from the only person who could have objected to such a move. Contrary to what God wanted for him, he heeded his wife's advice. The consequence of that advice is still the source of the unending wars in some parts of the world.

Practical Application
Many times, the easy way out of difficult circumstances may appear harmless and only a temporary measure. More often than not, it boomerangs. Examples include doing just anything to obtain permanent residence status of a nation.

Jeremiah to The Rechabites (Jer. 35:1-8).
Jeremiah was a renowned prophet of his time. People who disobeyed his warnings, prophecies were dealt with accordingly. The Rechabites on the other hand believed strongly in what they had been instructed in by their father. Even when a reputable prophet instructed them to do what was contrary, they refused. The obedience of the Rechabites was rewarded (Jer. 35: 18-19).

Practical Application
As children of God we are expected to obey him. God's word should have the final say in our life. Any advice, message, prophecy that contradicts God's word should be rejected irrespective of the personality of the person involved.

Questions

1. God used the man of God from Judah miraculously to demonstrate his power to Jeroboam, but he still died a shameful death. What does this mean to you in your Christian journey?

2. Propose ways in which the young man of God could have saved himself from this untimely death

3. In a family setting, how can we reject wrong advices and still not hurt one another?

4. What is the relationship (if any) between the spoken and written word of God?

5. How can we differentiate between true and false prophecies?

Conclusion.

The man from Judah died despite having accomplished God's purpose in the life of Jeroboam. The Rechabites who had no birthright to priesthood got in because of their obedience even under pressure. It does not matter how long you have known and served God, if you disobey him you may loose it all, including the salvation of your soul. If you choose to obey and surrender your life to Jesus Christ you are guaranteed a place in the kingdom. No matter how reputable the source of any advice, if it is not in keeping with God's word it is not for you.

Prayer

Give me a discerning spirit to differentiate who is truly sent.

Daily Bible Reading

1. Nehemiah rejected the counsel to run to the temple for the wrong reason (Neh. 6:10-14).

2. Shechem and his people agreed to be circumcised for the wrong motive; it became a snare to their slaughter (Gen. 34:1-29).

3. We are grafted branches, if we disobey, we can easily be removed (Rom. 11:11-25)

4. Many false teachings will arise in the later days (1 Tim. 4:1-6).

5. The devil is going around seeking whom he may devour (Job 1:7, 1 Peter 5:8-10)

6. Zerubbabel rejected the offer to help them build the temple because he perceived it was for a wrong purpose (Ezra 4:1-5).

NOTES

6

PASSIONATE PURSUITS

Text: 1 Corinthians 9:15-23

Memory Verse:
"Therefore I run thus: not with uncertainty. Thus I fight: not as one who beats the air."
(1 Cor. 9:26, NKJV)

Focus
To impress upon us that passion is required in order to achieve one's goals and to suggest ways of becoming passionate about what we do.

Definition:
The Merriam Webster dictionary defines passion as a strong liking or desire for or devotion to some activity, object, or concept. Passion is the drive to fulfillment of a purposed task. It is the bridge between accomplishment and failure. Passion separates doers from dreamers. It makes the simple to accomplish great things.

Introduction
Passion was evident in the life of Paul, though he was not alive at the time of Jesus Christ, he accomplished more than the apostles who walked with Christ. He set the goal of making heaven for himself and he strived passionately to make it. He did not take his calling for granted but put in his best in order to win the prize. Paul compares our needed passion to that of athletes – they give their games all it takes to win trophies. So anyone who wants to achieve greatness must vigorously pursue it with the intent of making it and being the best.

How To Bring Passion Into Your Pursuit To Achieve Greatness

A. **Define what you want to do**

You must be clear as to what precisely you want to do. Clarity of purpose makes focus easy. It prevents unnecessary diversion of effort and resources.

Nehemiah had a clearly defined purpose: to rebuild the walls of Jerusalem (Nehemiah 2:4).

B. **Do what you love best**

Minimal effort is required to get at what you love to do. More so, you strive to do those things better. When you pursue what you love you are more motivated and innovative.

C. **Develop a zeal for what you set out to do**

All accomplishments start from a desire. Your desire will determine the effort you put into what you have to do, which eventually determines the end result. Weak desires will produce weak results. Your desire will eventually determine your destiny (John 2:13-17).

Paul zealously became all things to all men in order to save some and bring them to the knowledge of Christ (1 Cor. 9:22).

D. **Be willing to pursue your desire with or without support.**

It is easier to accomplish things with support. However, a passionate person must be willing to achieve his goals with or without someone else. "If you follow your passion instead of others' perception you can't help becoming a more dedicated, productive person" (J. Maxwell).

David seemed estranged from his siblings because of his zeal for God's house (Ps. 69:7-9).

David single-handedly fought Goliath because his mind was made up that no one would defile the army of God (1 Sam. 17: 37, 45-47).

Questions

1. What are your passions as a child of God?
2. Passion separates doers from ----------------------.
3. Zeal must be with ---------------------- (Rom. 10:2).
4. What are some possible hindrances that may occur in our pursuits even when we have passion?

Conclusion

Irrespective of how good a plan is, without passion for what you are doing it is difficult to accomplish what you want. In the same token, if you do not have a passion for heaven you are likely to fall by the wayside. Start applying your heart to all you do and you will experience tremendous success in Jesus name. Amen.

Prayer

Lord help me to strive for excellence in all that I do.

Daily Bible Reading

1. David's desire to build the temple (1 Chro. 28:1-6, 29:1-5).
2. The church was determined that Peter must be released from prison, so they prayed fervently for him (Acts 12:1-18).
3. The early disciples desired to receive the Holy Spirit after Christ's resurrection (Acts 1:4-8, 2:1-4).
4. Solomon desired to get the wisdom (1 Kings 3:1-14).
5. Elisha was determined to receive a double portion of Elijah's anointing (2 Kings 2:1-15).
6. A reprobate mind: a result of evil passion (Rom. 1: 21-32)

References
The 21 Indispensable Qualities of a Leader by John C. Maxwell.
Let Go of Whatever Makes You Stop by John L. Mason.
Jesus, CEO by Laurie Beth Jones.

7

PASSIONATE PEOPLE AT WORK
Text: Ruth 1:6-18

Memory Verse:
"Whatever your hand finds to do, do it with your might; for there is no work or device or knowledge or wisdom in the grave where you are going."
(Eccl. 9:10, NKJV).

Focus:
Show some examples of people who were passionate about what they did.

Introduction
Since the stories in the Bible are for our examples, it is important to learn from the examples of various people who have lived before us. Some of these people were passionate about what they did and were able to achieve greatness in life. Let us learn from them.

Moses
Leading a self-sufficient nation requires wisdom. More so, a nation just freed from slavery, going on a wilderness journey, depending on God who they cannot see. Such was the enormous task Moses faced. His passion to have the people delivered from slavery to the promise land gave him the grace to bear with them through the difficult journey.

He prayed when fire struck the camp (Num. 11:1-3).

He sought to die in place of the people dying when he could not meet their need (Num. 11:15)

He pleaded with God to heal his sister, who openly spoke against him (Num. 12: 1, 9-13).

Practical Application:
Passion will make a difficult task accomplishable. It makes opposition appear like another opportunity to exercise patience. It puts achieving the goal above any unpleasant circumstance.

Phinehas (Num. 25:7-13)
Phinehas was zealous for God's righteousness in the camp. He killed those who committed grievous adulterous act that brought plague on the children of Israel. He thereby averted judgment from the congregation.
Practical application:
- Passion for God's kingdom will make us hate sin.
- It will make us seek God's face in repentance so that any trouble sin has brought into our lives may be averted.
- Like Phinehas' household, the covenant of peace and eternity with Christ will be ours forever.

Nehemiah (Neh. 2:17-20)
He was passionate about rebuilding the wall of Jerusalem. He sought resources, mobilized the people and surmounted all opposition.
Practical Application:
Passion will envision success when others see difficulty. It will transcend any barrier to supply of resources. It will create innovations that will accomplish the mission. Whatever you set out to do is accomplishable if you are passionate about it.

Henry Ford of Ford Motors (extracted from Entrepreneurs in Profile). Although Henry Ford was not a biblical character but we can learn about the passion that led him to success.
Ford in 1885 had the insight to what would later become a big automobile company. He wanted to make motorized car so cheap that the average person could afford it. He had many failed businesses by the age of forty. His neighbors thought he was a day dreaming mechanic. The company where he worked offered him a superintendent position, if he could give up working on his gasoline engine, rather than accepting this position, he went into business himself. By the age of fifty he had become one of the

richest people in the world. The success of Ford motors is still evident today. Henry ford believed "**failure is a chance to begin again more intelligently**".

Practical application
Passion will make you believe in your ability to accomplish what others cannot see. It will teach you to reject seemingly good offers that do not contribute to your purpose. It makes you to see failure as a learning process rather than defeat.

Paul (2 Tim. 4:6-8)
He stated how passionately he was pursuing his goal at all cost and God rewarded him with success as a champion among soul winners.

Jesus (John 14:1-6)
He is passionate about bringing many people into glory. He gave up all His glory just to share heaven with us. He sacrificed His own soul that we may live with Him eternally.

Practical Application
Passion will forgo comfort to accomplish the goal. Passion sees the glory beyond every discomfort and sacrifice required to achieve the goal.

Questions
1. Moses was passionate for ---
2. According to Henry Ford failure is -----------------------------
List some of the things passion for something will make you do.

Conclusion
Although Paul had a good spiritual training, he did not allow pride to motivate his work. He continued to fight and strive for the glorious crown of life with all fear and trembling. See beyond the present and go for the goal – you will win.

Prayer
Lord grant me the grace, passion and patience required to accomplish my goals.

Daily Bible Reading

1. Ezra determined to seek God and to teach the people His laws (Ezra 7:1-11, Neh. 8:9)
2. David was passionate to recover all that Amalek had stolen (1Sam.30:1-25)
3. Elijah; zealous for God, he destroyed the prophets of Baal (1 Kings 18: 20-40)
4. Mary Magdalene had a great desire to see the Lord (Luke 24:1-12)
5. The people who brought the paralytic man for healing had to make way through the roof to have access to Jesus (Luke 5: 17-25)
6. The Synophonenian woman was determined that her child must be healed (Mark 7: 24-30)

THE PEACE OF GOD
Text: Ps. 119:162-168

Memory Verse:

"Peace," I will leave with you, My peace I give you; not as the World gives, do I give to you. Let not your heart be troubled, neither let it be afraid."
John 14:27

Focus:

- To learn the ways to acquiring and maintaining God's peace
- To learn that the absence of God's peace can be chaotic
- To learn that God's peace is available and can be with great results

Introduction:

Peace means quietness, calmness, or freedom from war and disorder. It is something the whole world needs and craves for. Although the world does not know how and from whom to obtain it but the Bible says, God is the giver of Peace, and He gives it freely. All you need to do is to be willing to obtain it.

❖ **Foundation For God's Peace:**
  - Salvation in Christ Jesus (Rom. 5:1)
  - God's word (Ps.119:165)
  - Obedience to God's commandments (Is.26:3)
  - Trusting in God (Pro. 3:5-6)

❖ **Ways To Retain God's Peace**
  - Steadfastness in God's service (1 Cor. 15:58)

- Accept His forgiveness and forgive others (Matt. 19:27-30)
- Trust in His leadership for our lives (Pro. 3:5-6)

❖ **Result of Gods' Peace**
  - It lasts forever (John 14:27)
  - Nothing offends those who have God's peace (Ps. 119:165)
  - Easily live in Peace with men (Rom. 12:18

❖ **The Absence of God's Peace**
  - Causes absence of Peace with men
  - Brings bundles of problems
  - Cuts life short

Question

If you do not have God's peace is it easy to maintain peace with other people?

Conclusion:

Among things that money cannot buy is God's peace. No man has it for sale. It is only God that gives peace through Christ Jesus. God's peace is a lasting one. It will interest you to know that the power and grace to acquire it is within our reach. Let us rise therefore to acquire it. We will be glad we did.

Prayer

Let me experience your true peace Lord.

Daily Bible Reading

1. The peace with God (Rom. 5:1-5)
2. The Peace of God (Col. 3:15-17)
3. The Social peace (Rom. 12:15-21)
4. False peace at the absence of God's fear (Jer. 6:10-15)
5. To be spiritually minded is life and peace (Rom. 8:1-8)
6. Peace through healing is in Christ (Is. 53:1-5)

9

HOW TO ACQUIRE GOD'S PEACE

Text: John 14:25-31

Memory Verse:

"Peace I leave with you, My peace I give to you; not as the world gives do I give to you. Let not your heart be troubled, neither let it be afraid."
(John 14:27, NKJV)

Focus

- To broaden the understanding on God's peace by attempting to answer all questions in the study.

- Learn how to use various Bible translations to help improve understanding of a subject.

Quiz: Complete each of these sayings with the appropriate word:

I'm ready to throw in the ....
I'm at the end of my ....
I'm just a bundle of ....
My life is falling ....
I'm at my wit's ....
I feel like resigning from the human.............

The Three Kinds Of Peace

Fill in the blank with help from quoted Bible passage
1. _____ PEACE (This is peace with God)
    "Therefore, since we have been made right in God's sight by faith, we have <u>peace with</u> God because of what Jesus Christ our Lord has done for us." Romans 5:1 (NLT)

2. _____ PEACE (This is the peace of God).
"Let the peace of Christ keep you in tune with each other, in step with each other. None of this going off and doing your own thing. And cultivate thankfulness." Col. 3:15 (Msg - The Message Bible)

3. _____ PEACE (This is the peace with other people).
"Do everything possible on your part to live in peace with everybody." Romans 12:18 (TEV - Today's English Version)

The 5 Keys To Acquiring God's Perfect Peace

1. **God expects me to obey His _____ found in His word.**
"There is lasting peace for those who love your teachings. Nothing can make those people stumble." Psalm 119:165 (GW) *"I have obeyed your written instructions. I have loved them very much."* Psalm 119:167 (GW-God's Word)

2. **God expects me to accept His _____.**
"There is no other God like you, O Lord; you forgive the sins of your people who have survived. You do not stay angry forever, but you take pleasure in showing us your constant love." Micah 7:18 (TEV) *"God is faithful and reliable. If we confess our sins, he forgives them and cleanses us from everything we've done wrong."* (1 John 1:9 GW)

3. **God expects me to focus on His _____.**
"You will keep in perfect peace him whose mind is steadfast, because he trusts in you." Isaiah 26:3 (NIV)

4. **God expects me to trust in His _____ for my life.**
"Trust in the Lord with all your heart. Never rely on what you think you know; Remember the Lord in everything you do, and he will show you the right way." Proverbs 3:5-6 (TEV)

5. **God expects me to ask for His**_____.
"Don't worry about anything; instead, pray about everything. Tell God what you need, and thank him for all he has done. If you do this, you will <u>experience God's peace</u>, which is far more wonderful than the human mind can understand. His peace will guard your hearts and minds as you live in Christ Jesus." Philip. 4:6-7 (NLT)

Conclusion

The peace of God can only come from our knowledge of Him. Living our lives for Christ and totally depending on His leadership brings us divine peace that cannot be bought. Peace is a fruit of righteousness. May your peace be like a river in Jesus name.

Prayer

✓ Let your convenant of peace remain with me today.
✓ Lord, let my household dwell in peace.

Daily Bible Reading

1. Peace is a blessing from God (Ps. 29: 1-11).
2. Seek peace with others as much as possible (Rom. 12:18, Ps. 34:11-14).
3. Peace is a convenant of God when I obey His commandment (Is. 48:18-19).
4. Peace of God also comes with peace with men (2 Sam. 16:5-13, 19:15-20).
5. Isaac did not argue with the Phillistines, he remained connected to God, and he was blessed (Gen. 26:12-23).
6. The work of righteousness is peace (Is. 32: 9-20).

NOTES

JEALOUSY
1 Samuel 18:1-9

Memory Verse:
"Wrath is cruel and anger is a torrent, but who is able to stand before jealousy"
(Prov.27:4 NKJV).

Focus
- To understand what jealousy is.
- To find out why people become jealous.
- To learn how to deal with jealousy.

Definition:
Jealousy is an inner feeling of resentment of someone's success, achievements, and potentials. It is a disposition of exclusive possession of someone /something that results in watchful guarding of the thing. More often than not, there will be a corresponding outward display of the resentment in various forms.

What Are the Causes of Jealousy?
1. **Insecurity**: Saul did not like the victory ascribed to David (1 Sam. 18:6-9), and he felt insecure about the throne. From that time on he disliked David. Instead of benefiting from David as a man of war, Saul spent time seeking to kill him.

2. **Outside Influence**: As Christians, when we are privileged to achieve outstanding records, glory is to be ascribed to God not man. Situations that result in comparing individuals' achievements should be avoided.
   People can also influence one into developing a spirit of jealously against the other. If those women had not sung

their song, Saul might not have gotten jealous. The Jews also tried to arouse jealousy in John's mind by telling him that Jesus also was baptizing in John 3.

3. **Immaturity**: When people feel they are not accorded due right (2 Sam. 19:40-43). The people of Israel felt they were despised in not being invited to bring the king over the Jordan. John responded with maturity in John 3 and avoided jealousy, but Saul acted immaturely and allowed jealousy.

4. **Unfulfilled desire**: Rachel became jealous of her sister because she bore no children (Gen. 30:1).

5. **Insincerity**: When a wife commits adultery, the husband becomes jealous (Pro. 6:34, Num. 5:12-14). The same applies when the husband commits adultery.

6. **Inferiority Complex**: When someone else seems to be preferred over us (Gen. 4:4-7, 37:3-4). Cain was jealous because God had respect for his brother's offering, not his. Joseph was more loved than his brothers.

7. **When people forsake the source of their provision**, you provoke the person to jealousy. God made abundant provision for Israel and cared for them as the apple of His eye (Deut. 32:10-14). When they became satisfied, they forsook God, and served other gods provoking Him to jealousy (Deut. 32:15-21).

Practical Application:
Many Christians are faithful in serving God when they seek his face for blessings. As soon as they receive their heart desire, they become too busy to make it to fellowship. Sunday becomes an ideal day to wake up late and get to church any time. Their tithe is too much for the church where they worship. The church becomes inadequate to accommodate their newly achieved status. Before they realize it, their heart is turned to other means of

sustenance. We may just be on the same route the Israelites took provoking God to jealousy. The question, however, is can we pay the price? Should God withdraw His blessings so that we can truly return to Him?

8. **Misplaced priority**: When others receive what you believe you are entitled to (Deu.32: 21, Rom. 10:19, 11:11). God would provoke Israel to jealousy by His dealing with another nation.

Questions
1. Why do people become jealous?
2. How can we deal with jealousy?
3. Is it right to be jealous over spiritual things? e.g. spiritual gifts in the lives of others.

Conclusion:
It is obvious that no one else can deal with jealousy in our lives except we ourselves. Therefore, let us take steps to get rid of its roots in our lives.

Prayer:
Father, I uproot jealousy in my life and I replace it with the spirit of love in Jesus name.

Daily Bible Reading:
1. Jealousy is evidence of carnality (1Cor. 3:3)
2. Jealousy is an unbecoming behavior in the life of a Christian (Rom. 13:13)
3. The qualities of love (1 Cor. 13:1-8a)
4. We must prefer others to ourselves (Rom. 12:9-16)
5. Continuous trusting and faith in the Lord will bring our blessings (Joel 2:23-27)
6. Minding spiritual things more than the things of the flesh will save us from jealousy (Rom. 8:5-14)

11

CONSEQUENCES OF JEALOUSY
Text: 1 Samuel 18:10-26

Memory Verse:
*"Wrath is cruel and anger is a torrent, but who
is able to stand before jealousy"
(Prov. 27:4, NKJV).*

Focus
- To discuss some of the problems that could occur as a result of jealousy.
- To have more understanding why jealousy is evil.

Introduction
Jealousy when not promptly handled always leads people to carry out actions that may have grievous consequences. That is why it is essential to handle any feelings of jealousy quickly before it deteriorates.

Outcome of Jealousy

A. **Hatred: Joseph** was hated by his brothers (Gen. 37:2-5) because their father loved him more than his brethren. The hatred was so profound that they could not tolerate him to be superior to them in any way.
   - As Christians we should not create enmity between our children by treating one more favorably than the others..
   - Where you sense some atmosphere of jealousy, be careful not to reveal your plans carelessly.

B. **Murder:** (Gen. 4:8) Cain killed Abel, because he was preferred to him.

C. **Unnecessary fear:** Saul became afraid of David for no just cause (1Sam. 18:14-16). Instead of Saul to keep on enjoying the benefits of the skill of David, he lived in the bondage of fear. Jealousy will make us slave to fear rather than beneficiaries of someone's skill. The fear was more of guarding his position than God's people being delivered at battle.

D. **Deceitful life:** Still in a plot to kill David, Saul pretended he genuinely wanted to give his daughter Michal to David in marriage, but actually he was hoping that David would die by the hand of the Philistines (1 Sam. 18:17-26). When you are jealous of someone, you cannot deal truthfully with the person. You will use acceptable things to cover the wickedness in the heart. Unfortunately, God sees our heart and we will be judged accordingly.

E. **Seeking the downfall of others**: The satraps in Babylon sought hard to find a fault against Daniel, so that he may lose his position in the kingdom, just because they envied the excellent spirit in him (Daniel 6:1-5). Jealousy has created unhealthy atmosphere in churches, with people seeking the downfall of others with an excellent spirit. Rather than benefit from the anointing on such people, they look for ways to discredit them.

F. **Revenge:** Jealousy that arises when a husband feels betrayed by the wife usually ends in disaster. There is no relenting until the person takes revenge (Pro. 6:34-35).

G. **Unhealthy Competition** Rachel and Leah despite being sisters forgot all about blood relationship. Rather than enjoying their husband, they tried hard to out perform each other. While in a bid to have the upper hand, they went to the extent of giving their maids to their husband. Jealousy will cause anyone to lose sense of good reasoning. Instead of proffering solutions, they increased the number of wives that Jacob married (Gen. 30:3-9).

Question:

How can people kill one another using their tongues as weapons?

Conclusion:

It is reasonable to be content with things that we have according to the scripture in Heb. 13:5

Prayer

Every deceitfulness in my life as a result of jealousy please forgive me.

Daily Bible Reading:

1. Better is little with the fear of the Lord (Prov. 15:16-18)
2. Godliness with contentment is great gain(1 Tim. 6:6-10)
3. Learn to trust and rest on the Lord and commit thy way to Him (Ps. 37:3-7)
4. Joseph was hated, but never hated back (Gen. 45:1-7)
5. If there is no covetousness, there will be no jealousy (Ps. 119:33-37)
6. Live by the Word of God, it keeps from sin (Ps. 119:125-131)

12

PREVENTING JEALOUSY
Text: Luke 15:21-32

Memory Verse:
"A relaxed attitude lengthens life; jealousy
rots it away"
(Prov. 14:30, NLT).

Focus
To learn how to prevent living a jealousy-controlled life.

Introduction
The effect of jealousy is not just mental, but as our memory verse indicates, it rots away and thereby cuts one's life short. As you know, rottenness is not pleasant and is results to gradual decay with a worthless end. Therefore, it is better to prevent jealousy than to deal with its attendant effects.

How To Prevent Jealousy.

A. **Do not compare yourself with others:** Everyone is a unique creature of God. We are made by Him, for Him and His pleasure. We are fearfully and wonderfully made (Ps. 139:14). If you want to be like someone else you will not only be displeased with where you are now, but you will never appreciate what God has brought you through. Instead of comparing yourself with others, measure yourself based on set goals and where God wants you to be. Such assessment gives you joy in what you have achieved and hope for improvement (Gal. 6:4-5). Paul made this clear to the Corinthians that no one is superior to the other (1 Cor. 3:5-9).

B. **Love yourself:** As simple as it may sound, loving yourself is the key to loving and accepting others. If you

46

love yourself, you accept who you are, you appreciate what you do and you will be grateful for where you are. As such, you are able to love your neighbor and not be jealous of who they are or what they have attained (Matt. 22:37-39). Many at times jealousy is borne out of the projection of disapproval of oneself.

C. **Rejoice with those who are blessed before you.** When you rejoice with others you open the door to your own blessing (Rom. 12:15)

Recognize when jealousy arises and handle it promptly:
- Realize that jealousy is a spirit. Renounce it and repent of it in your prayers (Num. 5:14). If Cain had promptly yielded to God's advice he would not have gotten to the extent of killing his brother (Gen. 4:4-7).
- Be content with whatever you have and be willing to use whatever talent you have for others (Heb. 13:5-6).

Questions

1. How do you resolve the paradox of using your talent and others becoming jealous
2. How do we recognize jealousy?
3. How does loving yourself help you to love others?
4. In what ways can we compare jealousy to be as cruel as the grave?
5. What other idols in our lives can provoke God into jealousy?
6. How should siblings deal with jealousy within the family?

Conclusion:

Let us be satisfied with who God made us to be and appreciate who we are. This is because God has made all things well; including you and I. He even said: WE ARE VERY GOOD (Gen.1:31)

Prayer

Lord, help me to love and accept myself just as you have made me.

Daily Bible Reading:

1. Whatever you want others to do to you, do it also unto them (Math. 7:12)
2. Hating one self can lead to suicide; so love yourself! (Matt. 27:1-5)
3. Man was created to rule and dominate. No chance for jealousy (Gen. 1:26-31)
4. Look unto Jesus, Not on the things of others. (Heb. 12:1-2)
5. Jealousy is as cruel as the grave (Song of Solomon 8:5-6)
6. Never provoke God into jealousy by serving any idol (Ps. 78:53-64)

13

HARDENED HEART

Text: Hebrews 3:7-11

Memory Verse:

"Blessed is the man who always fears the Lord,
but he who hardens his heart shall fall into
trouble"
(Prov. 28:14, NIV).

Focus:

To know causes and gravity of heart hardening and learn how to use God's word to liberate the hardened heart.

Introduction:

When something is hardened, it is difficult to cut through, mold or change its form. A hardened heart cannot easily perceive God's word. It is difficult to get access to such a person; neither can they utilize God's word for any transforming process. Such people hold firmly to what they think or believe and are unyielding.

Causes of Heart Hardening

1. **Unbelief** (Ps. 95:8-9, Heb. 3:12):
   The Israelites could not relate God's previous deliverances and provision to immediate need. They constantly grumbled against Moses for anything they lacked. Unbelief does not allow our hearts to appreciate any good God has done. It makes us hardened to God's unlimited ability. Hence, God perceived Israel's hardness of heart as an act of unbelief.
   Practical Application – Consider areas in your personal life that you have faced challenges. Do you believe God for any change at all? Or your heart has become resilient to God's ability.

2. **Trivializing what is wrong:** This is making attempts to justify what is wrong or making "reasonable" excuses for wrong doings. Saul assumed not carrying out God's total instructions was not a "big deal" (1 Sam. 15:7-15)

3. **Deliberate blockage or rejection of what is right:** Eli's sons deliberately did not listen to the correction of their father. (1 Sam. 2:22-25)
When we deliberately shut off the Holy Spirit we become insensitive to His voice. At that time we follow our own ways.

4. **Associating with wrong people** (1 Kings 12: 8-11, 1 Cor. 15:33): Rehoboam, the king, decided to take the advice of his peers at the expense of the advice of elders who stood before his father Solomon. Instead of taking to the wisdom of the elders, he answered the people roughly when the whole assembly of Israel came to him to reduce their burden.

5. **Being overtaken by deceitfulness of sin** (Heb. 3:13): Sin can be so deceptive that many at times even supposed Christians fall into the trap. A present day example is the approval of homosexuality by some as norm. When we fail to recognize and accept sin for what it is, the heart becomes hardened to that particular sin.

6. **Failure to align with God's purpose and plan:** Once relieved from plagues Pharaoh failed to let the Israelites go (Ex.8: 12-14). When people refuse to align with God's purpose, He gives them over to their heart's desire, till they are finally destroyed (Roman 1:28, 2:5). Many people have turned down God's plan of restoration and salvation. They are seeking other means to please God. Jesus, however, is the way.

7. **Insistence on having things one's way** (Matt 18:8-9):
Sometimes we deviate from God's original plan by our actions. As in the case of divorce, it brings a negative impact on those involved. Insistence on one's way is not

scriptural for the Bible says; we should not be wise in our own eyes (Pro. 3:7).

8. **Pride**, which usually precedes destruction (Pro. 16:18).

Questions
1. The final outcome of a hardened heart is --------------------
2. People fall prey of sin because sin can be -------------------
3. Is there any relationship between a hardened heart and rebellion? If yes what is the relationship?

Conclusion:
Hardness of heart develops gradually not overnight. The only antidote to this subtle problem is to daily exhort ourselves in the word of God (Heb 3:13). The Bible has made it clear that pride goes before destruction (Pro. 16:18). Today, if you hear His voice, do not harden your heart.

Prayer
Lord, give me a heart of flesh.

Daily Bible Reading
1. Unbelieving heart is an evil heart (Heb. 3:7-14).
2. Unbelief always prevents people from receiving their blessing (Heb. 3: 15-19).
3. Salvation and submissive heart can only be found in Jesus (Acts 4:10-12).
4. Do not harden your heart (Ps. 95: 8-11).
5. Hardened heart leads to continuous disobedience (1 Sam. 13:8-15; 15:16-23)
6. God will not despise a contrite heart (Ps. 51: 7-17).

NOTES

14

PLEASANT WORDS

Text: Proverbs 25: 11-13

Memory Verse:

*"Pleasant words are like honeycomb, sweetness to
the soul and health to all the bones"
(Pro. 16:24 NKJV)*

Focus

To appreciate the role of pleasant words in relationships.

Introduction

What we hear goes a long way to affect our response and subsequently our behavior. Honey is a thick sweet liquid produced by bees. It is naturally sweet and does not require special processing prior to consumption. When something is pleasant, it is nice, lovely, enjoyable, satisfying and agreeable. Hence pleasant words will be naturally sweet to the ears, satisfying to the hearer and attract one to the speaker. The medicinal effect on the body of the hearer cannot be underestimated nor overemphasized.

Effects of Pleasant Words

- It causes rejoicing in the innermost being (Pro. 23:16). When there is deep-seated rejoicing, it reflects on the immediate surrounding, with a welcoming atmosphere.

- Pleasant words cause a magnetic pull to the speaker.

- It can neutralize any impending trouble (Pro. 15:1).

- It heals wounds not causing new ones (Pro. 12:18).

- It has profound effect on the health of the hearer (Pro. 16:24).

Practical Application
Consider the beautiful and wonderful orations given at burials. Seldom do you witness any burial ceremony where people say unpleasant words about the deceased. During the lifetime of some of the people all they have heard is how they are good for nothing and how they cannot make it in life. Some have lived their lives verbally abused. Many suicides have occurred in the lives of depressed people who have never heard pleasant words. Marriages have broken down because one spouse says the other is no good. Children have committed murder because of recurrent unpleasant words from their colleagues. Have you ever considered that if pleasant words bring health to all the bones, many more people could have lived longer lives if they heard pleasant words? Could marriages be salvaged if everyday both parties speak pleasant words to one another? Can children who are wayward be made to retrace their steps with pleasant words of hope?

What is the best source of pleasant words?
God's words are the best source of pleasant words that are sweet like honey.
- David claims God's words are sweeter than honey (Ps. 119:103).
- Ezekiel ate the scroll and he likened it to honey (Ezek. 3:3).
- The Israelites ate manner and it was like wafers made with honey (Exo. 16:31).

Questions
1. What if I need to give a piece of my mind to somebody? Will I not be pretending?
2. If one keeps speaking pleasant words to one's spouse, won't one be taken for a ride?
3. What if the person I speak pleasantly to does not reciprocate in like manner to me?
4. I have already spoken unpleasant words to someone what should I do now?

Conclusion

If God's words are the best source of pleasant words, then I need to study His words so that I become a reservoir of pleasant words. My life must be surrendered to him completely, so my heart can change for his goodness. Make up your mind from today to consciously speak pleasant words to your spouse, children, relatives, brethren and colleagues on daily basis. See how many lives you can bring healing to their bones and lengthen their days by your pleasant words. God will give you the grace. You can do all things through Christ that strengthens you.

Prayer

God grant me the grace to speak pleasant words to someone daily.

Daily Bible Reading

1. Pleasant words may be few, but are gracious (Eccl. 10:11-15).
2. Abigail words averted David's intention to destroy the house of Nabal (1 Sam. 25:13-28).
3. Pleasant words should always be used in communication between spouses (Song of Sol. 2: 8-13).
4. Sound speech saves from enemies (Titus 2:7-8).
5. Spiritual songs are full of pleasant words, so sing to the Lord and to ears of men (Eph. 5:17-20).
6. Let your words always be seasoned with salt (Col. 4:5-6).

15

SIN

Text: Ezekiel 22: 1-13

Memory Verse:
"Therefore, to him who knows to do good and does not do it, to him it is sin."
(James 4:17, NKJV)

Focus:
To explain the concept, meaning and the root of sin.

Introduction:
Pastor Kayode Ige once said, "Sin is **Satan's Identity Number**." The word sin alone is used 346 times in the OT & 127 times in the NT. It is so rampant that only the grace of God helps one to live as a living sacrifice.

Definition:
According to McClintock and Strong Encyclopedia, "SIN is any action, word, desire, purpose, or omission contrary to the law, of God; a voluntary violation of, or failure to comply with, the divine law (Rom. 3:20; 4:15; 7:7; James 4:17)."

The concept of sin
Sin carries the following connotation in the Bible:
Rebellion & Lawlessness – 1Sam. 15:23, Jer. 5:23-25
Perversion & immorality – Gen. 39:9
Evil – Gen. 50:17
Breaking God's laws – 1 Jn. 3:4
Being unkind. Matt. 25:41-46
Living in ways contrary to the will & nature of God – Rom. 1:32; Gal. 5:19-21, Rev.21:8
Not worshipping God, as we should – Matt. 4:10, Rev. 14:7.

Not loving our Lord with all our heart, mind, soul & strength. – Matt. 22:37-40

Not loving our neighbor as ourselves – 1 Jn. 3:15-16

Doing the things we shouldn't & omitting what we should – Jms. 4:17

The origin of sin

1. **Sin began with the Rebellion of Satan and some angels in heaven (Isaiah 14:12-14)**. Lucifer (Satan) was endowed with ability to sing. When he sang, it was as if many instruments were playing. He felt so elated and wanted to be like God. Hence he rebelled against God. Rebellion is a sin, which will be treated in details in a later study in this book. As Christians we should be careful of this type of sin.

2. **Sin Begins from the heart.** The heart is the 'battle ground' where every thing takes place *(Ref. The Way, Vol. IV)*. Everything is conceived there *(James 1:13-15, Jer. 17:9)*.
   "But those things which proceed out of the mouth come forth from the heart; and they defile the man. For out of the heart proceed evil thoughts, murders, adulteries, fornications, thefts, false witness, and blasphemies:" (Matthew 15:18-19).

3. **Sin began in the world by Adam and Eve's rebellion.** (Genesis 3:6-7). Eve saw the tree was good. It appeared pleasant to her. It generated a desire in her heart. She shared the 'good fruit' with her husband. Instead of becoming the parents of righteousness, they became perpetrators of sin *(Rom. 5:12)* Sins will start by appealing to the sight, and then the heart becomes involved when we linger on the thing. When it is finally conceived in the heart, the action is carried out. From this story, sin tends to spread out of our 'love' for close ones. This explains why close friends will be involved in fraud, illicit drugs, sexual immorality etc. Man will offer the 'good fruit' to their 'loved' ones. This calls for caution as to the type of 'good' offers we accept.

Question

1. Are all sins punishable?
2. Will things done for survival be counted against the person?
3. Are all sins rectifiable? Back up your answer with scriptural examples.

Prayer

✓ God help me to surrender all to you.
✓ Help me to stop trivializing what I need to repent of.

Conclusion

Men over time have tried to reduce the impact of sin on their conscience, calling it trivial things such as a mistake, one of those things, survival instincts, the norm, etc. whatever we choose to call it, does not change God's view of sin. When we trivialize sin, it prevents us from repenting. May we not miss heaven in Jesus name. Others have viewed sin by the gravity of the offense, of the opinion that judgment will vary according to sin. The truth however is that sin will not be allowed in heaven. It is time to repent.

Daily Bible Reading

1. Whoever is born of God does not sin (1 John 5:16-21)
2. When things are done without conviction of God's approval it is sin. (Rom. 14:14-23)
3. In the last days many sins will become evident 2 Tim. 3:1-7
4. God in His wrath against ungodliness gives people up to do whatever they please till final judgment (Rom. 1:18-24)
5. If you do not love, you are not of God (1 John. 3: 10-14)
6. Current righteousness will not cancel future transgression (Ezek. 33: 12-20).

Reference

McClintock and Strong Encyclopedia, Electronic Database. Copyright © 2000, 2003 by Biblesoft, Inc.

16

EFFECTS OF SIN ON A CHRISTIAN

Text: Psalm 51:1-end

Memory Verse:
"But your iniquities have separated you from your God; and your sins have hidden His face from you, So that He will not hear"
(Isaiah 59:2, NKJV).

Focus
To understand the effects of sin in the lives of Christians and find biblical answer to overcoming sin.

Introduction
Easter is about celebrating the risen Christ. The purpose of His resurrection is to deliver us from sin and its consequences. As we rejoice in the liberty of deliverance from death to life, make sure the reality of Christ's resurrection is found in your personal life.

Effects of sin on a Christian

1. **Sin makes one unclean** and thereby separates us from God (Ps. 51: 2, 7, 10). David repeatedly asked to be cleansed. Sin makes us not to be presentable to God. God cannot behold unclean things. God does not accept unclean worshipers. We ought to present ourselves unto God as living sacrifices, holy and acceptable (Romans 12:1-2).

2. **Sin fills one with guilt:** This makes it difficult for us to concentrate on godly things. Our prayers are greatly hindered when our minds are full of guilt. Meditating on the word becomes almost impossible when our minds are guilt-ridden. (Ps. 51:3-9)

3. **Sin can affect one's health**: Sin is the worst joy killer. In fact it does not only kill joy, it brings sadness. The process of guilt that begins with guilt feeling ends up in depression – which is a deadly sickness. David was so depressed that he could hardly function. (Ps. 51:8)

4. **Sin affects our worship (communion with God):** Sin blocks the flow of the Holy Spirit, destroys communication between us and God and denies us communion with Him. Sin denies us the liberty of worship and locks our mouths, our hearts and our spirits. The sacrifice of praise cannot be offered on an altar of corruption (Ps. 51:14-15).

How to overcome sin
- Keep a strong personal relationship with the Lord Jesus Christ (Acts 17:28).
- Apply the blood of Jesus daily (Eph. 1:7).
- Live a life of forgiveness (Col. 3:13).
- Appropriate the word of God (John 15:7).
- Pray daily (1 Thess. 5:17).

Prayer
- ✓ Give me a humble heart to admit when I sin against you.
- ✓ Let the purpose for which Christ was crucified not be in vain in my life.

Conclusion
The whole purpose of Easter is Jesus has been offered as a sacrifice for sin. As you celebrate, have you truly accepted the lamb that was offered on the cross for the atonement of your sin? Church membership does not translate to accepting Jesus as Lord and Savior. Surrender to Him today, just as you are and the whole essence of Easter will be a reality to you.

Daily Bible Reading
1. Christ died for us while we were yet sinners (Rom. 5: 6-11).
2. God forgives our iniquities, not dealing with us according to our sins (Ps.103: 1-10).

3. If we confess our sins God will forgive us (Ps. 32: 1-11).
4. If the mind is unclean, whatever we offer is unclean (Haggai 2: 10-14)
5. You will be responsible for the consequence if you do not yield warning (Eze.33:1-11)
6. If the righteous turns away into wickedness, his righteousness shall not be remembered any more (Ezek. 33: 12-20)

17

WATER BAPTISM

Text: Matthew 28:19-20

Memory Verse:

"He who believes and is baptized will be saved; but he who does not believe will be condemned."
(Mark 16:16, NKJV)

Definition:

What is Baptism? Baptism is a rite of purification involving "a decisive commitment to a personal piety." [*Dictionary of the Bible, J.D. Douglas, p69*]. There are two (2) types of baptism: (a) Water Baptism and (b) Holy Spirit Baptism, but this study will focus only on water baptism.

Focus

To understand the essence of water baptism in a Christian's life.

Introduction:

Water Baptism is the act of being immersed into water and raised up again after one repents of his or her sins and accepts Jesus Christ as Lord and Savior. This is a person's first step into the Christian life. After this act of repentance (Mat. 3:11) follows the continuous in- filling of the Holy Spirit as He makes one dead to sin and gives grace to live holy. Through Holy Spirit baptism the redeemed sinner is incorporated into the spiritual body of Christ.

Why is Baptism necessary?

1. It is the commandment of Jesus (*Matthew. 28: 19-20).* Jesus Himself did it; although He had no sin, He set Himself as an example for all of us to follow (Matthew 3:13-17).

2. It signifies death to sin and resurrection to holiness in Christ. The meaning and efficacy of water baptism can best be understood only in the light of the redemptive death and resurrection of Christ. So as Jesus likened his death to baptism in Luke. 12:50 and Mk. 10:38, so must you show the world that you are dead to sin and resurrected to holiness. Jesus put upon himself all our sins, died and was buried with the load of our sins. On the third day he rose again. So must you signify your love for Christ by dying and being buried to your sins [by being immersed into water] and being raised into a new life in Christ Jesus [by being raised up from the water]. By faith, the blood of Jesus mixes with the water the Lord Himself blesses it to wash your away sins.
3. It gives outward and visible signs of our declaration to live for Christ (Lk. 8:36 & Acts 10:47).
4. It signifies inward regeneration (Jn. 3:3,5). You must be born again.
5. It prepares one for the baptism of the Holy Spirit (Mat. 3:11), this does not preclude Holy Spirit baptism prior to water baptism.

Prerequisites for Baptism:
1. Confession of sins and acceptance of Jesus Christ as Lord and Savior (Mt. 3:6). Though baptism of repentance was done prior to the cross, Jesus is now the only acceptable sacrifice for the forgiveness of sins.
2. Repentance (Acts 2:38)
3. Faith (Mk. 16:16, Acts 8:36-37 & Acts 18:8)
   Once these are present, you are qualified to be baptized. Then the church will take you through a baptismal preparatory class in order to (1) to prepare you for the step-by-step events of the baptismal process, (2) reiterate to you that it is a biblical requirement, and (3) prepare you for what you will experience as you become a full member of the body of Christ. Only the Pastor, Evangelist, or any other pastoral designate shall conduct baptism.

** It is essential for anyone who is professing Jesus as their Lord and Savior to fully know and understand what they are confessing. As such, it is not advisable to baptize anyone less than twelve years of age, so as to ascertain proper understanding of their knowledge of salvation.**

Where should the Baptism take place?

Based on the examples left for us by Christ, John the Baptist, and many disciples, our church recognizes only the baptism that is conducted by immersion.

How is the Baptism administered?

At the place of Baptism, the Pastor, Evangelist, or ordained designate shall ask you again if you accept Jesus Christ as your Lord and Savior. Upon your confession that you accept Christ as your Lord and Savior, you shall:

1. Be immersed into the water (Mk. 3:16), once (not 3 times).
2. In the name of God the Father, the Son, and the Holy Ghost (Mt. 28:19).

Once you are raised up again, you are now a new person in Christ and you are recognized as a full member of the church (Acts 8:33 & 39).

Do I need to repeat baptism?

If at the time you joined the church you have been baptized in a different church, your baptism shall be deemed valid as long as it was done by immersion. However if your baptism was not by immersion, you should request to be baptized again in accordance with the method stipulated above. John the Baptist immersed converts and Christ Himself was immersed. Both the Greek and Hebrew translations of the word "baptism" suggest dipping or immersion.

Who could be baptized?
1. Individual – as the Eunuch in Act 8:38 and Paul in Acts 9:18
2. Household – Stephanas' household in 1 Cor. 1:16.
3. Group – as many believers in Mat. 3:5-6 and Acts 18:8

Questions
Explain the difference between water and Holy Spirit baptism.
If I was not previously baptized by immersion what do I do now?

Conclusion:
Please note that there is only one baptism – unto repentance in Jesus alone (Eph. 4:5). Once you've been buried to sin and raised to life in Christ; the evidence of being born again must now begin to show forth in your life (Romans 6:14).

Prayer
Lord, help me to live a life worthy of what my baptism symbolizes.

Daily Bible Reading
1. The Ethiopian eunuch though read the scripture, needed understanding of what he was reading, which led to the salvation of his soul before he was baptized (Acts 8:26-39).
2. Fruits worthy of repentance are essential, not just the outward show of baptism (Luke 3:1-9).
3. Lydia and her household were baptized (Acts 16:14-15).
4. The baptism of John was not man made (Mark 11:27-33).
5. Water baptism is not all that is required, we need to be baptized in the Holy Ghost (Acts 19: 1-7)
6. We are all baptized into one Lord (Eph. 4:1-5)

18

HOW TO OVERCOME WORRY

Text: Luke 12: 22-25

Memory Verse:

*"Therefore do not worry about tomorrow, for
tomorrow will worry about its own things.
Sufficient for the day is its own trouble"
(Matt. 6:34, NKJV).*

Focus

To understand how to overcome worry.

Introduction:

Many Christians profess to believe God, however when situation beyond their control arises, we panic, worry and literally forget the God we professed when all was well.

What is worry?
Worry is a state of being uneasy, apprehensive with anticipation of terrible things. It is a state of restlessness produced by personal or others assessment of uncertainty of situations. Worry usually creates uneasiness, expectation of the worst. You cannot pinpoint precisely what is wrong at times. It is uneasiness or distress about future uncertainties.

What causes worry?
- trying to mentally or emotionally get into the things that are not here yet, or have already been
- facing the devil or the enemy on your own. This occurs when you leave God in the today and go on your own into tomorrow or when you return to yesterday (Mt 6:34, Mt.6:11, Heb. 11).
- lack of faith (Mt 6:28, Phil. 4:19)

Why Should I Avoid Worry?
- God has a plan for you to prosper (Jer. 29:11)
- Because anxiety weighs people down (Proverbs 12:25)
- Worry will not change anything (Mt. 6:27)
- Worry drains one's strength (Nehemiah 8:10)
- Worry drives one out of the presence of the Lord (Ps 16:11)
- Phil. 4:6-7 says be not anxious for anything.
- Worry can cause sickness e.g. Heart attack, high blood pressure, ulcers etc.

How Can I Prevent Worry? (Mt. 6:33)
- Avoid seeking God for just what He can give. Begin to seek the kingdom of God and provision will become your reality. When you trust God for everything you cannot worry.
- Let us imagine how we feel when we realize that people just love us for what we are giving them but not for whom we are. It implies that the person really loves the comfort and privileges that your money affords not you. In the same token, many people are serving God for what they can derive from Him, not genuine love for Him.
- Learn to live one day at a time.
- Be content with what you have (Heb. 13:5)

How Can I Recover From Worry?
Recovery and freedom is only found in the Word of God (John 8:32). Therefore put more of God's words into your soul and the word will encourage you and help you redirect your focus away from worries to faith and good expectations.
- Learn that the only requirement to praise God is the breathe you have (Ps. 150)

Questions
Is worry a sin? See Mt. 6:25.

Prayer
Lord remove my worries and help me to cast all my cares upon you.

Conclusion
There is nothing we brought into the world. In the same token there is nothing we are going to take out. So why not learn to enjoy whatever you have been privileged to get now, instead of dwelling on what you have not yet acquired.

Daily Bible Reading
1. The Israelites were worried and grumbling about what to eat. Exo. 16:1-end
2. Anxiousness is against the will of God (Phil. 4:6-7)
3. Don't get worried about tomorrow because each day has enough trouble for itself (Mt. 6:34)
4. Anxiety can cause depression (Pro. 12: 25).
5. It is better to have little with God's fear (Pro. 15:16-17,17:1)
6. Ability to enjoy the fruit of your labor is the gift of God (Eccl. 5: 13-20).

19

TIME TO SWEETEN YOUR MARRIAGE

Text: Song of Solomon 4:1-5

Memory Verse

"Wives, submit to your own husbands, as to the Lord. For the husband is head of the wife, as also Christ is head of the church; and He is the Savior of the body. Therefore, just as the church is subject to Christ, so let the wives be to their own husbands in everything.

Husbands, love your wives, just as Christ also loved the church and gave Himself for her, that He might sanctify and cleanse her with the washing of water by the word"
(Eph. 5:22-26, NKJV).

Focus

- To teach that everyone has an emotional need that must be filled.
- To discard the notion that some people are unlovable
- To highlight the languages of love
- To emphasize practice rather than complaint.

Introduction

According to Gary Champan "At the heart of mankind's existence is the desire to be intimate and to be loved by another. Marriage is designed to meet that need for intimacy and love".

God from the beginning of life ordained the institution of marriage. It was originally meant to be a perfect union between a man and a woman. It was ordained for mutual companionship, help and comfort. More often at marriage ceremonies we hear the

Pastor say "Dearly beloved, we are gathered here before God and this congregation to join this man and this woman in Holy Matrimony which is an honorable estate established by God before the fall of man ..." The intention of God is that we live happily ever after, but our neglect, insensitivity, lack of discernment and selfishness created the woes we suffer, the pains we endure and the bitterness we transfer to our innocent children.

Everyone has an emotional tank, i.e., an emotional need that has to be met. If we leave our emotional tank unfilled it could lead to emotional drifting, unfriendly response, irritation and rudeness.

How to Spice up Your Marriage
Dr. Chapman in his book "The Five Languages of Love" has identified five different ways to communicate and accept love. This lesson is based on his teachings.

A. **Words of Affirmation**: This is simply saying kind words to your spouse as often as the opportunity avails itself if that is his/her love language. You will be surprised the energy such kind words will generate in your marriage. The Bible says *"pleasant words are like a honey comb, sweetness to the soul and health to the bones."* Proverb 16:24 and 1st Corinthians 8:1b. Everyone wants to be loved. You build up your partner and elevate his/her vitality through praises, kind words and verbal expression of love. Proverb 12:25 says *"Anxiety in the heart of man causes depression, But a good word makes it glad".* "Verbal compliments are far greater motivator than nagging words".

"Verbal compliments or words of appreciation are powerful communicators of love. They are best expressed in simple, straightforward statement of affirmation".

Practical

How many times have you used any of these phrases for your spouse this year?

Phrase	Never	More Often	Can't Remember
1. Oh! My, my, you look good today;			
2. You are the best thing that has ever happened to me;			
3 I really appreciate your support in my project;			
4. Thank you for scrubbing the bathtub;			
5. I really appreciate the way you've being taking good care of me and the children;			
6. It is really thoughtful of you to fill my tank with gas;			
7. Thank you for the food it really tastes good.			

How to Compliment Your Spouse

1. **Encouraging Words**: This is an act of motivating and inspiring your spouse. Help your spouse to develop his/her potentials, you can say something like- you are a good writer. You are such a good cook.

2. **Kind Words**: "Love is kind, we are to communicate love verbally, and we must use kind words. Our spouse will usually interpret our message based on our tone of voice, not the words we use". I encourage you to show your spouse some caring and nurturing. Speak to them with soft voice, not yelling or shouting. Love also does not keep record of the past, it does not bring yesterday's problems or failures into today because that will pollute the wonderful day that God has given us. (1 Cor. 13:4-5)

3. **Humble Words**: "Love makes requests and not demands". Love wins where arrogance and demand fails. Be considerate with your spouse. For example say "I love the way you cooked the fresh fish last week, is it possible you can cook it again this week?" rather than say "it seems we are only going to be eating fresh fish once a month, I wonder why I work so hard all day." 1 Peter 3:7.

"When you make a request of your spouse, you are affirming his or her worth and abilities. You are in essence indicating that she has something or can do something that is meaningful and worthwhile for you. When you make a demand you become a tyrant not a lover". Example of humble words is: Honey, could you help me to pick my coat from the cleaner? This is different from you must not come home without my coat from the cleaner.

Questions
1. How do you discover the primary love language of your spouse?
2. Does one's language change over time?

Conclusion
There is power in words. The Bible confirms this in Proverbs 16:24 that pleasant words are pleasant and healthy to the bones and of course – your marriage. The more kind words you speak the more love you get.

Daily Reading
1. Rhythm of love (Song of Solomon 1:1-end)
2. Descriptions of love (Song of Solomon 2:1-end)
3. Longing for one's beloved (Song of Solomon 3:1-end)
4. A word for the wife (1 Peter 3:1-6)
5. A word for the husband (1 Peter 3:7-12)
6. Dealing treacherously with one's spouse (Malachi 2:10-17).

20

PUTTING LOVE INTO PRACTICE
Text: Song of Solomon 4:1-5

Memory Verse
*"... Because the LORD has been witness between
you and the wife of your youth, with whom you have
dealt treacherously; yet she is your companion and
your wife by covenant"
(Mal. 2:14, NKJV).*

Focus
- To emphasize the essence of spending quality time with
  one's spouse.

Introduction
Many spouses know what works in marriage but not all spouses
put it into practice. It is however not enough to know the
principles that work but we must know to work them.

Quality Time
Sharing your time and undivided attention with your spouse and
forsaking every other thing is crucial to your marriage's joyful
survival. Spending time together and making him or her your
priority is very important in showing love to your spouse. This
type of activity should be deliberate and at the same time
spontaneous.

Marriage could be likened to a baby; it needs nurturing and care.
Quality time spent together is the vitamin required to stimulate
marriage from infancy to adulthood. The genesis of most
marriages over 15 years old that collapsed is the failure to create
a communication pattern before the children left home. Couples
often grow apart unknowingly. Songs of Solomon 7:11-12.

Quality time requires intentionally spending time with your spouse. You cannot say that you are giving your spouse an absolute attention when you are engulfed in CNN, ABC or FOX programs. Some spouse often complain that their spouse love the T.V or surfing the Internet than they love spending time with them.

Practical

How many times have you practiced any of the following this year with your spouse:

Phrase	Never	More Often	Can't Remember
1. Hold each other			
2. Take a deliberate walk together			
3. Go out for lunch/dinner.			
4. Take a weekend off out of town			
5. Stay home while children are in School			
6. Attend Church Convention out of town			
7. Gone to banquet together			

How to Observe Quality Time with Your Spouse:

1. **Togetherness**: "A central aspect of quality time is togetherness". This does not mean physical propinquity. Two people could be riding a car, or out to lunch together, but not together. "The importance of this is to spend focused time with each other physically and emotionally. This shows that we care about one another and that we enjoy being with each other, that we like to do things together." (Ephesians 5:29-32)

2. Quality Conversation: "This means sympathetic dialogue where two of you are sharing your experiences, thoughts, feelings and desires in a friendly, uninterrupted context. This focus on what we are hearing not what we are saying". This involves maintaining eye contact, listening with feelings and uninterrupted attention.

3. Quality Activities: "Quality activities include things that one or both of you have interest in. The purpose is to experience something together" i.e. listening to music, taking long walk, washing car together, going to the movies, etc.

Questions
What if we are not interested in the same things what do we do?
What if I get bored easily, how can we spend quality time?

Conclusion
You are encouraged to stop analyzing your spouse, but to look at your marriage as a relationship and invest love and time in it. Let your concern be how to create a loving atmosphere for your spouse. God puts love into practice and he is our best example. God's attitude toward us is always one – positive.

Daily Bible Reading
1. Doing it God's way (Ephesians 5:22-26).
2. What love is (1 Cor. 13:4-10).
3. It is better to marry than to burn (1 Cor. 7: 1-9)
4. Two are better than on (Eccl. 4:9-12)
5. Practicing the act (Genesis 26: 6-9)
6. Take time out for just the two (Song of Solomon 7: 10-13).

Acknowledgment:
Dr. Chapman's Book; "The Five Languages of Love" was used extensively in this two series study.

Read "His Needs, Her Needs" – by Willard F. Harley Jr. & "Love" – by Kenneth Hagin

21

TRINITY

Text: John 14:6-11

Memory Verse:

"For there are three that bear witness in heaven; the Father, the word, the Holy Spirit, and these three are one" (1 John 5:7, NKJV).

Focus:

Shed light on the doctrine of Trinity
Show the reason why we Christians believe in Trinity

Introduction:

The word "Trinity" is used to explain the eternal relationship between Father, Son and Holy Spirit. The word itself is not in the Bible, so is the word "Bible" used to described the word of God. Trinity is hard to explain with words because the existence is beyond our imagination. It is extremely difficult to find anything in our normal earthly experience that exists in trinity, and this makes it very difficult to conceptualize. This concept can only be accepted by faith.

What is Trinity?

Trinity means God (single being) in three persons (existing simultaneously as three distinct persons). God the Father, God the Son and God the Holy Spirit. There is only one eternal Godhead (Deut. 6:4; Isaiah 44:6; 1 Cor.8:4) and this God is in three persons who maintain co-existence, co-equality in nature, power and attributes, contratry to some opinions claiming that christians serve three Gods. There is only one God in three divine persons. Although they are distinguisable, (i.e. the Father is not the Son and Son not the Holy Spirit), but they are indivisible in attribute, power, nature and glory. The central, and crucial affirmation of Christian faith is that there is one savior, one God, and one salvation. We have access to the Father through the Son (Jesus Christ) by the help of the Holy Spirit (John 16:23)

Why do Christians believe in Trinity?
They all bear witness in heaven: The Father; the Word(Son) and the Holy Spirit (1 John 5:7-8).

The three divine persons showed up in action during Jesus baptism: Father's voice from heaven; Son being baptised and the Holy Spirit decending like a dove (Matt 3:16-17).

Father sends Holy Spirit in Son's name (John 14:26).

The word which was in the beginning, became flesh and dwelt among us (John 1: 1-5, 14).

A Perfect communion is revealed in 2 Cor.13:14 where we read "Grace of Lord Jesus Christ, love of God, and fellowship of the Holy Spirit..."

We see baptism into the three divine persons in Matt 28:18-20 as the Son instructs us to baptize "...in the name of the Father, and of the Son, and of the Holy Spirit.

We have acess unto - the Father; through the Son, by the Spirit (Ephesians 2:18).

Questions:
What is the special characteristic of each Person?
How can you prove that the Holy Spirit is a Person?
The Holy Spirit has a mind, will and emotions. Rom. 8:26-27; 1 Cor. 12:11

Conclusion
Jesus has been raised to meet our every need, it pleases God to ordain Jesus as our redeemer and that all the fulness of God to dwell in His son. This means that Jesus is the only way to reach the Father. As earlier written in this study, the doctrine of triune can only be accepted by faith and as we know faith comes by hearing and hearing the word of God.

Daily Bible Readings

1. Personality of the Holy Spirit: Gen. 1:2; 6:3; Luke 12:12; John 15:26; 16:8; Acts 8:29; 13:2; Rom. 8:11.

2. The Holy Spirit is God: Acts 5:3-4; 2 Cor. 3:16-18 *Eternal - Heb. 9:14; *Omnipresent (present everywhere) - Ps. 139:7;   *Omniscient (all knowing) 1 Cor. 2:10-11; *Ominipotent (all powerful) Lk. 1:35

3. The Holy Spirit is involved in all of the works of God
   *Creation: Gen. 1:2; Psa. 104:30
   *Birth of Jesus: Matt. 1:18, 20; Luke 1:35
   *Resurrection: Rom. 1:4; 8:11
   *Salvation: Rom. 8:1-27

4. The three divine persons revealed (Revelation 4 – 5).

5. The nature of God: God is a Spirit (John 4:24); God is light (1 John 1:5); God is love (1 Jn. 4:17 & Heb. 12:29).

6. What are the symbols of the Holy Spirit? John 7: 38-39; Matt. 3:11; Acts 2:2; Luke 10;38

References:
Foundation of Christian Doctrine – Kevin J. Conner
Christian Research Institute
PC Study Bible Commentaries.

22

MYTHS AND FACTS ABOUT TRINITY

Text: John 14: 18-26

Memory Verse:
"He was in the beginning with God"
(John 1:2).

Focus
Clarify some of the misundertanding about Trinity

Introduction
The Christian Research Institute states that "Many modern groups teach a nontrinitarian understanding of God. These include but not limited to The Church of Jesus Christ of Latter-day Saints, the Jehovah's Witness, the Christadelphians, Christian Scientist, the Unification Church, Unitarian niversalists, American Unitarian Conference, Branhamist, Frankists and Oneness Pentecostals. If they speak of the Trinity at all, they represent it as consisting of the Father, the man Jesus, and a divine influence—the Spirit of God."

Some people claim:
1. **"Jesus is not God"** but the Bible says:
   o God called His Son (Jesus) God (Heb. 1:8-9).
   o Without Him (Jesus) nothing was made (Jn. 1:3).
   o God spoke about Jesus' perpetual existence from the begining (Heb.1:10-12).
   o He was begotton not created (Heb. 1: 5).
   o He is self existing (John 5:26 Amp.).
   o His name is Mighty God (Isaiah 9:6).

2. **"Jesus is lesser than God"** but the Bible affirms:
   o The fullness of God is in Christ (Col. 2:9-10)

- o Supremacy of Christ (Col. 1:15-17)
- o Equality in attributes and honor (John 10:30 & 5:23)
- o The authority to judge the world (2 Cor. 5:10)
- o Power to forgive sins (Lk. 5:21,24)

3. **"Jesus is just a Prophet"** but the Bible affirms:
   - o He is higher than other prophets and does not need sacrifice for personal sins (Heb. 7:26-28).
   - o He is the firstborn of every creature (Col.1:15, 18).
   - o He was before Abraham (John 8:58).
   - o He came from heaven not from dust (1 Cor.15:47).

Questions
What other myths have you heard about the trinity?

Conclusion
The Bible from the passages sited above establishes the supremacy of the Lord Jesus Christ. Irrespective of what people say, think or believe, it does not change the fact that Jesus is Lord. Accept Christ now, He is waiting eagerly to receive you.

Daily Bible Readings Readings
1. Jesus will do whatever we ask Him that the father may be glorified (John 14:12-15).
2. Godliness is a great mystery (1 Tim. 3:14-16).
3. Jesus was with the father and had glory before the world was (John 17: 1-5).
4. The world was made through Him (John 1:1-10).
5. Jesus was in the form of God (Phil. 2: 5-11).
6. The father and the son are both to be honored (Jn.5:16-23).

References:
Foundation of Christian Doctrine – Kevin J. Conner
Christian Research Institute
PC Study Bible Commentaries.

NOTES

23

FEAR

Text: Jeremiah 1: 4-10

Memory Verse:
"For the thing I greatly feared has come upon me, and what I dreaded has happened to me"
(Job 3:25, NKJV).

Focus:
To enumerate different types of fear that people experience.

Introduction:
This study is not referring to the fear of God or the respect one gives to the elderly. Job's fear was unfounded because God's gifts and his calling are irrevocable (Rom.11: 29). The gifts and callings are without repentance.

Class Participation
1. How do you experience fear as a person?
2. How do you deal with it?

What is Fear?
Living in expectations of the worst coming to pass (Job 3:25). It is living in danger, whether real or imagined. It is the absence of confidence or certainty. It is also to doubt God's ability to deliver one from danger or unpleasant situations.

Different types of fear:
Fear of failure: Saul and his army were afraid of losing the battle at the threat of Goliath (1 Sam. 17: 4-10). Instead of facing the battle, they fled from Goliath (1 Sam. 17:24). Fear would weaken anyone's strength. It cheapens skill and kills initiative. Trained men of war became weaklings at the thundering of Goliath's

voice. They forgot they were covenant children and could depend on God.

Practical Application:
Many business ideas, laudable projects, visions and goals have been prematurely terminated for fear of failing. The greatest failure that anyone can have is never starting at all. Mistakes can occur even with the best plans, however, they should be used as opportunities to learn and maneuver, not as reasons for quitting. God had already made provision for us to rise if we fall (Pro. 24:16). As Christians we should not rejoice at people's failure (Pro. 24:17).

Fear of the unknown: The Canaanites were afraid of what could become of their nation because of what they heard God did for the Israelites with other nations (Josh. 2:9-11).

Fear of death: The Israelites were afraid of dying at the red sea when Pharaoh pursued them (Ex. 14:10-13). They preferred to have remained slaves than to die in the wilderness. Fear of death can hold people bondage in unpleasant circumstances instead of embracing God's deliverance for a better future.
Peter denied Jesus for fear of the outcome if he revealed his identity as a follower of Christ (Matt. 26: 69-74). Fear of death has made people deny the faith. Some have hoped that they will have a chance to ask for forgiveness, which may not always be available.
Adonijah was afraid Solomon would put him to death; he, therefore, sought a safe haven by taking hold of the horns of the altar (1 Kings 1:50-53). Thank God Adonijah knew the right place to seek for solace. Not everyone run for deliverance in the right place. Fear of death has driven many to seek security in occultism, wrong advisers, false prophets that have cost some the salvation of their souls.

Fear of man: Elijah was afraid of Jezebel's message so he ran for his life (1 Kings 19:1, Prov. 29:25, Heb. 13:5-6). What will man say or think?

Fear of others' reaction: The chief rulers who believed in Jesus did not want to confess him for fear that the Pharisees might put them out of the synagogue (John 12: 42-43). Many Christians today are afraid of confessing Christ for fear of losing friends, popularity, gains etc. If we deny him on earth He will also deny us in the kingdom.

Fear of lack: This has made some people devote all their time and energy to making enough to make ends meet at the expense of serving God (Matt. 6:31). The unfortunate thing is that they wear themselves out, without really making it to the top (Eccl. 10:15).

Fear of the enemy: Elisha's servant was afraid when he saw the host of chariots sent to capture his master. (2 Kings 6: 14-17). He became confused as to what to do. Thank God for Elisha, who understood God's divine protection better. As a child of God you do not run from the enemy, you are empowered to overcome him.

Fear of circumstances: Peter became afraid when he saw the boisterous wind around him (Matt. 14:30). He felt he was going to sink. As Christians, many at times we become fearful when faced with the storms of life. We remove our focus from the Lord like Peter did, and things appear to be falling apart. If only we would look around us and see that Christ is still where we left Him. We are the ones who have changed direction.

Fear of rejection: Moses was afraid of being rejected by the Israelites in Egypt. He gave several excuses for his inability to accomplish God's purpose (Exo.3: 11-13, 4:1). Excuses at times give an inner sense of justification for what ought to be accomplished. People have self-made barriers such as age, gender, ethnicity, language, physical strength etc. which have greatly limited what they could have accomplished.
Fear of sickness (Job 3:25)

Conclusion

The final outcome of fear is to incapacitate the individual and prevent actualization of full potential. Fear has torment. If you have identified any form of fear you have, it is time to overcome such. Jesus was manifested to destroy all the works of the devil. Remember that fear is the policeman used by the devil. Resist his arrest by standing firm on God's word.

Prayer

✓ Everything that has terrorized my life Lord put an end to them in Jesus name.
✓ Whatever I have lost as a result of fear, help me to win them all back.

Daily Bible Reading

1. Fear of death caused David to tremble (Ps. 55: 4-8).
2. Joshua and the Israelites were not to fear the nations they were to take over their land (Deut. 31:1-8).
3. The shepherds were afraid when they saw the angel that came to break the good news of Jesus birth (Luke 2:1-15).
4. Jesus came to conquer death (Heb. 12:14-end).
5. Fear not (Isaiah 41:1-end).
6. Fear, even when Jesus was physically present (Matt. 4:35-41).

24

DELIVERANCE FROM FEAR

Text: Psalm 118: 6-17

Memory Verse:

*"The Lord is on my side; I will not fear: what can
man do unto me"
(Psalms 118:6).*

Focus

- To learn the basis and consequences of fear.
- To learn how to be delivered from fear.

Basis of fear

When we think God cannot handle the situation.

When help appears not to be forth coming (1 Sam. 28:4-7).

When things depart from the pattern we are used to.

When God's mighty works are forgotten with the rising of the slightest oppression (Is. 51:13).

Feeling of incompetence (Jer. 1:6).

When people feel helpless about confronting situations of life.

What is the outcome of fear?

a. It will rob you of your faith. (Mark 9:24)

b. It will rob you of your joy. The children of Israel spent more time weeping in the wilderness, than they did thanking God for their deliverance from slavery.

c. It will rob you of your miracle. (Matthew 14:28-30)

d. It will rob you of your inheritance. In the case of the twelve spies, ten returned with a negative report because of fear while two spoke positively with boldness. The spies were leaders from their various tribes. Had they not been fearful of what they saw, they would have gotten to the peak of leadership amongst the people. (Num. 13:1,26-33)

e. It will make you settle for less than God intends for you. The Israelites wished they were left alone to remain slaves in Egypt instead of facing death in the wilderness (Exo.14: 10-12).

f. Hostile, aggressive behavior: King Saul threw a javelin at David (1 Sam.18: 10-13).

g. Fear of being hurt. This will result in being defensive, self-protective, and intolerant of criticism or correction.

What should I do to be delivered from Fear?

a. Remember that even the one threatening you is a man that will also die (Is. 51:12).

b. God will come to your rescue (Is. 35: 3-7).

c. Present the confronting situation to God in prayer (2 Kings 19:14-18).

d. Recognize that fear is Satan's weapon. What does the Bible say about weapons? (Isaiah 54:17)

e. Confess the word of God. (2 Tim. 1:7)

f. Christ has conquered death (1 Cor. 15: 55-57).

Questions
Is fear merely a thing of the mind?

Conclusion
God has not given us the spirit of fear but of love, power and sound mind. Therefore begin to realize that greater is He that is in you than he that is in the world (1 John 4:4, 2 Tim. 1:12). Begin to face your fear facts e.g. do things you were hitherto afraid of doing. Being filled with the Holy Spirit will also help destroy fear (Acts 4:23,24).

Prayer
Lord, please deliver me from the spirit of fear and timidity.

Daily Bible Reading
1. Fear is a natural result of sin (Gen. 3:10; 4:13-14; Prov. 28:1)

2. Fear makes people attempt to hide from God (Gen 3:8; Rev 6:15-17)
3. Fear belongs to unbelievers (Matt 10:28; John 3:18)
4. Wicked people fear the righteous (Prov 28:1; Matt 14:5; Rom 13:3)
5. It is the wicked who acts deceitfully (in fear), to hide evil (2 Sam 11; Matt 28:4-15).
6. Dismissed fear from your heart (Matt. 8:26; 10:26-28,31; Lk. 12:32)

References:
Nelson Bible Dictionary
International Standard Bible Encyclopedia

25

BUSY DADDY
Text: 2 Kings 4:18-24

Memory Verse
"Train up a child in the way he should go, and
when he is old he will not depart from it."
(Proverb 22:6, NKJV)

Focus
To teach that dad's involvement in the home should go beyond
provision.

Introduction
Thank God you made it to another father's day. It is good to have
children you are proud of in days such as this. Being a father
however is not without attendant responsibilities. You have to
provide for the entire household and nurture them in godly
manner. The story of the Shunamite woman is very familiar. She
was a respected woman that carried her husband along in
whatever she did. He presumably had the fear of God because he
supported her course in caring for the man of God (2 Kings 4:9).
He was a good example of a father who is easy going, God
fearing, able to provide for his house, but too busy to be fully
involved.

He did not perceive Elisha was a man of God (2 Kings 4:9).
When we are too engulfed with our activities, we do not have
enough time to communicate with God. Vital information we can
receive are not transmitted through our spirit. He could have
missed the link to him being a father through the miracle of his
son's birth that occurred by Elisha's pronouncement.
As a father, does your schedule allow for personal time to
fellowship with God? Or you are too busy, so that personal time
with God is on the 'run'? Thank God there was a helper who

could perceive the presence of a man of God. How much better would it be if both could perceive God's presence in their home.

He could not differentiate when to be involved from when to instruct (2 Kings 4: 19).

Busy dads do not have too much time on their hands to be distracted from their routine schedules. The man was busy with the reapers. His child's cry of discomfort only generated an instruction instead of instant involvement. He could not make time out from his reapers to attend to his only child. Hard work is good, but it should not be at the expense of the family. This father's only child died while he was still busy working, despite that he was there at the onset of the problem. Thank God it was Elisha's days; imagine if it was this century and the child needed immediate resuscitation (CPR), the golden first few minutes would have been missed because dad was too busy to take time off. "Its all for the family" dads say, but not taking time out for the people you claim to work for may cause more grievous problems. Remember God placed dad as the head, which is where most of the senses are located. Moreover Solomon says we labor and leave all behind not knowing how it is going to be spent (Ecc. 2:16-19).

He did not have enough time to extract from the wife what was wrong (2 Kings 4: 22-23).
A sick child was just taken away, mum comes soon after with an unusual request, yet dad provided all but himself and his time. Son dead, mummy saddling to the prophet at unusual time, dad is still busy with the reapers! Jesus did not stop at providing salvation; He gave us the Holy Spirit to remain with us so we can keep fellowship with Him. Dad's provision is wonderful and appreciated but dad's availability should complement his provision. Money will buy a house not a home. So dad, adjust your schedule to be more available.

Example of a busy dad

David was a man of war, valiant and brilliant king; yet he was too busy to be involved in raising his children. We can read some of the outcome of David's children:

Amnon raped his sister Tamar (2 Samuel 13:1-24).

Absalom rebelled against and attempted to dethrone his father (2 Samuel 15-18)

Question

1. Since dad is responsible for provision, how can he balance it with personal availability?
2. Suggest ways in which dad can get involved in the affairs of the house.
3. What impact does single parenthood have on children upbringing?

Conclusion

When dad is fully involved we can achieve better outcomes in the home. Please Dad, do not leave the upbringing of your children to Mum alone. Not only does your wife need your support, your children also need your leadership.

Prayer points

✓ I ask for forgiveness for all my negligence in the training of my children and I receive the grace to take responsibility in Jesus name.

Daily Bible Reading

1. Busy prophet with vile and unrestrained sons (1 Sam. 3:11-14).
2. Judah sons did wicked things for which they were killed (Gen. 38:6-10).
3. Judah had affairs with supposed harlot (Gen. 38: 11-23).
4. Laban was actively involved with raising his children (Gen. 29: 7-9).
5. Isaac & Rebekah preferential love for their children was not the best atmosphere to raise children (Gen. 27: 1-13).
6. One of the sons of the prophet feared God, but left his house I debt at his death (2 Kings 4: 1-2).

26

TEST YOURSELF

Vessels In the House

A. List what kind of vessels can be found in a great house according to 2 Tim. 2:20

1. _____
2. _____
3. _____
4. _____

B. The church, the assembly or congregation is the ----------------- house. The individual believer is the -------------------------------- A vessel of honor is anyone that uses the ---------------------- God has deposited in him/her.

C. For as we have many members in one body, but all the members do not have the same ----------------, so we, being many, are -------------- body in ------------, and individually members of one another. Having then ------------ differing according to the --- --------- that is given to us, let us use them: if prophecy,... (Rom. 12:4-8)

Vessels unto Honor

D. But we have this -------------- in ------------ vessels, that the excellence of the --------------------- may be of God and not of us. -----Cor. ------:7, NKJV.

E. Where in the Bible is this quotation from? "Nevertheless the solid foundation of God stands, having this seal, the Lord knows those who are His and let everyone who names the name of Christ depart from iniquity"

F. List four qualities of vessels of honor:

1_____

2_____

3_____

4_____

Caring For Ministers
Give two reasons backing it up with scripture reference why ministers should be cared for:

1. _____

2. _____

Reputable source, but bad Counsel
True or false: All advices from reputable source are represents the will of God _____.

Support your answer with one Bible example.

Passionate Pursuits
List four steps you can take/do to passionately pursue your desires:

_____

_____

_____

_____

Jealousy
"Wrath is ----- and anger is a -------, but who is able to stand before --------" (Pro.27:4 NKJV).

Give three suggestions on how we can overcome jealousy:

_____

_____

_____

Hardened Heart
What is the effect of trivializing what is wrong on our heart?

Pleasant Words
What effect has speaking pleasant words to people had on your home, job and relationships in general. Share a practical example.

Sin
Mention at least four things sin can do in the life of a believer.

Fear
Fear has torment. Explain this statement.
List some of the different types of fear and what effect each one mentioned has on our personal life.

Conclusion
Hope this testing section gave you an opportunity to revise what you have learnt earlier in the year. Much more, be a doer of the word.

Daily Bible Reading
1. Previous acts of righteousness shall not deliver in the day of transgression (Ezek. 33:12-20).
2. When you hear God's word, but do not take action the repercussions may come suddenly (Ezek 33: 30-33).
3. In the last days people will depart from the truth (1 Tim. 4: 1-5).
4. Continuity in doctrine is essential (1 Tim. 4: 12-16).
5. Hold fast to what you have learnt in Christ (2 Tim. 2: 13-14).
6. Endurance is necessary to please our master (2 Tim. 2: 1-7).

27

HYPOCRISY IN WORSHIP

Text: Galatians 2:11-21

Memory Verse

"This people draweth near unto me with their mouth, and honoureth me with their lips, but their heart is far from me"
(Matt. 15:8, KJV).

Focus

- To define hypocrisy and learn what constitutes a hypocritical behavior in worshipping God.

Definition:

The Oxford Dictionary defines hypocrisy as behavior in which a person pretends to have higher standards or beliefs than is the case. It is to falsely pretend to possess virtues. To pretend to be what one is not.

Introduction

Peter was one of the pillars of the early church, as such; he had great impact on many of the Jews who accepted Christ. Paul always accorded them recognition and had earlier gone to discuss with them (Galatians 2:1-10). In the gathering at Antioch, Peter ate with the Gentile Christians until other Jews came. Peter whom God had used to introduce Christ to the Gentiles withdrew from them when he saw other Jews. It created a scene that Paul had to openly rebuke him.

Actions that constitute hypocrisy in Worshipping God

- Israelites swore by God, but it was not in truth or in righteousness (Is. 48:1-2, Jer. 5:2).

- When people seek God daily, show enthusiasm in knowing his ways, but carry out His instructions with levity (Is. 58:1-5). This can also be likened to those who faithfully attend church activities without any transformations in their lives through the words they have heard.
- When we live in sin and pretend to be holy (Is. 65:4-5).
- When deliverance is viewed as an opportunity to do anything that pleases one (Jer. 7:9-12).
- When we have other gods in our heart, but pretend to genuinely seek the counsel of Jehovah (Ezek. 14:1-5).
- When we are hearers but not doers of God's words (Ezek. 33:31).
- When God is just one among several other gods that is worshipped (Zep. 1:5).

Questions

1. The Israelites set up gods in their _____ (Ezek. 4:4).
2. Mention other places in which people can set up gods.
3. Hypocritical worshippers show love with their _____ but their _____ go after _____ (Ezek. 33:31).

Conclusion:

God is genuine, anyone who must worship Him, must do it with genuineness of heart. If worship is done hypocritically, it amounts to a waste of time, energy, and service which is worthless and unrewarded. Let's not forget that God is also a spirit. He requires that all who would worship Him would do it in spirit and in truth (John 4:23-24)

Prayer

Lord, teach me how to worship in truth and in Spirit.

Daily Bible Reading

1. God will set his face against any man who sets up an idol in his heart and comes to inquire for his will (Ezek. 14:5-11).

2. No matter how precious, God will do away with anyone whom He corrects that refuses to change (Jer. 7:8-20).

3. If the worshipper is not clean, whatever that person offers is not acceptable (Haggai 2:11-14).

4. Herod wanted to kill Jesus, but presented himself as a worshipper to the wise men (Matt. 2:1-13).

5. Ability to quote scriptures does not represent true knowledge of Christ, because even the devil used scriptures to tempt Jesus (Matt. 4:1-11).

6. The Pharisees paid more attention to the outward ceremonial cleaning at the expense of inner growth (Luke 11:39-42).

28

HYPOCRISY IN SERVICE
Text: Luke 11:42-45

Memory Verse:
"And he (Amaziah) did that which was right in the sight of God, but not with a perfect heart"
(2 Chro. 25:2).

Focus
To learn the acts that can constitute insincerity in service to God.

Introduction
Service can be effectively rendered without genuine sincerity to God and the persons been served. It is possible to serve God with our lips and actions, but our hearts may be far from him. One may serve an organization with zeal and yet be insincere in one's heart.

Acts that constitute Hypocrisy in Service include:
1. Service to God rendered solely for gains (Micah 3:11).
2. Service rendered so as to be seen and acknowledged by others (Matt. 6:1-4).
3. Service rendered without complete obedience to God (Matt. 7:21-23).
4. Service rendered with an ulterior motive (Matt. 7:15).
5. Responsibility that is willingly accepted but not dutifully carried out (Matt. 21: 28-32).
6. Preaching the word of God without being an example of what is preached (Matt. 23:1-3)
   - A pastor who doesn't pay tithe.
   - A church leader who cannot manage his/her home.
7. When rules are made for the followers that the leaders are not willing to obey themselves (Luke 11:46)

8. When tradition is the basis for service as opposed to the leading by the spirit of God (Mark 7:1-5).

Questions

1. Give examples under each of the actions mentioned above.
2. Identify if any of these occurs or has occurred in the past in your life/group/church.
3. Proffer solutions to overcoming being a hypocrite in service.
4. What dangers do hypocrites pose to the church?

Conclusion:

Hypocrites will end up in hell, because they are not part of God. Therefore, let us serve in spirit and truth; not as unto men. It is of the Lord we shall receive the reward of inheritance (Col. 3:17, 23-24).

Prayer

Lord, please help and deliver me from wasted effort in service.

Daily Bible Reading

1. Hypocrites openly display their activities with God (Matt. 6:5-8).
2. The plight of prophets who make people err (Micah 3:1-8).
3. The Pharisees urged Jesus to speak more, not because they wanted knowledge, but they sought for an occasion to accuse him (Luke 11:47-54).
4. Traditionalistic people will reject God's commandment just to keep their tradition (Mark 7:9-16).
5. Reasonable service is to present ourselves as a living, holy and acceptable sacrifice unto God (Rom. 12:1-2).
6. God knows our works and service (Rev. 2:18-23).

29

HYPOCRICY IN RELATIONSHIP
Text: Genesis 29:14-28

Memory Verse:
"Therefore, whatever you want men to do to you, do also to them, for this is the law and the prophets"
(Matt. 7:12).

Focus:

To learn that:
- Hypocrisy in relationship has been in existence since Bible days up until now
- Hypocrisy in relationship has not been profitable to those who practiced it then and now
- To make up our minds and deviate from the act of hypocrisy in relationship.

Introduction

Relationships are valuable and a good name is to be chosen above great riches. The way we relate to one another in various settings of life is an indirect reflection of our state with God. Deceitful dealings with people are not without repercussions. Though we may not see the effect immediately, in the long run we pay for it.

1. **Jacob & Laban** (Genesis 31:38-41)
   As an employee of Laban, there was inconsistency in Jacob's wages. Several times it was changed. Many Christians are finding it difficult to engage in business deals with one another, for fear of being defrauded. This ought not to be so in God's household. Christian employers should not defraud employees. Neither should employees take their bosses for granted simply because they are Christians (Eph. 1 Tim. 6:1,2).

2. Samson

- Samson was an unfortunate victim of many hypocritical relationships. One wonders why he fell repeatedly into the traps set up for him.
- Samson & the woman in Timnath (Judges 14:15-17): For fear of death, Samson's first wife dealt deceitfully with him
- Samson & his friend (Judges 14:20,15:1-2)
  - The person who was originally his companion became his rival and later married his wife.
- Samson and Delilah (Judges 16:4-6, 16,18)
  - For the love of money, Delilah betrayed trust in a matrimonial relationship.

3. Jesus & Judas

Judas was a close ally of Jesus, one of the twelve of his time, the keeper of their account but he was not straightforward with the master. He ate with him from the same plate; hence we can assume he had a privileged position. Why did he have to betray Jesus for money? Could Judas not have gotten all he wanted from the purse?

Such is the superficial relationship among some brethren today. Despite the fact that they eat and dine with one another, backbiting is still very much rampant. Some Christians have used their privileged positions in various ministries to cause the disintegration of such ministries. If true relationship cannot be found in God's house, where should we go for it?

4. Jacob & Rebecca

Jacob & Rebecca dealt treacherously with Isaac (Genesis 27:2-21). In a nuclear family you would expect transparency in their dealings with one another. Instead, favoritism resulted in treacherous dealings in the same family.

5. Jacob & Esau

These were twin brothers who ought to be sincere with each other. Jacob, however, dealt craftily with his brother. He pretended to be Esau in order to receive his blessings. In today's terms, people are scared to give siblings money to help them in major projects, money designated for parents are intercepted by siblings. As children of God how do we prevent these things from infiltrating the church?

Lesson Learnt:

- The Timnite wife of Samson betrayed him out of fear of being killed by her people (Judges 14:15). In the long run, the same punishment she did everything to avoid finally came upon her and her household (Judges 15:6). There is always a consequence for the hypocritical person in a relationship.
- Judas hung himself (Matt. 27:5).
- Rebekah lost fellowship with her beloved son for years and not for a few days as she proposed (Gen. 27: 42-46).
- Jacob reaped what he sowed, in that he was deceived by Laban (Gen. 29:20-26).

Food for Thought

Check your motive for being involved in the ministry. Is it for good or otherwise?
What is the status of your relationship with your brethren?

Conclusion

We have seen hypocrisy in relationships in various settings: employee and employer, husband and wife, friends, leader and worker. It transcends all aspects of all. This implies that hypocrisy has to do with the individual, not the circumstance. The good news is that there is a friend who never fails. His name is Jesus. He can guide you in your relationships. Though betrayed, it was not without his knowledge. Let Him help you through your relationships.

Prayers

God help me to value relationships.
Lord, teach me to maintain integrity in all relationships.

Daily Bible Reading

1. Delilah carries out each plot against Samson (Judges 16:6-15)
2. Joab with others planned to help Adonijah to the throne, at the expense of their loyalty to David (1 Kings 1:1-7)
3. Cain killed is brother and asked God whether he was his brother's keeper (Gen. 4: 1-10).
4. Do away with unfaithfulness, the cause for which Christians have not been free with each other (Lam. 3:22-25, Ps. 40:10-11).
5. The lives of hypocrites end among perverted persons (Job 36:5-14).
6. Joseph was hated by his brothers, sold to slavery and a lie was told to their father that Joseph was killed by a beast (Gen. 37: 8-36).

30

YOUTH AND SEXUALITY

Text: 1 Cor. 3:16-20

Memory Verse:

*"A prudent person foresees the danger ahead
and takes precautions; the simpleton goes blindly
on and suffers the consequences"
(Proverbs 22:3).*

Focus

- To compare God's design for sex with society's idea of it.
- To show and explain the physical, emotional, and spiritual consequences of premarital sex.
- To explain abstinence as the way of life in our everyday lives as Christian youth.

God's Original Design for Sex

- Humans did not create sex, God did, and because of that, God is the only one who understands it best.
- In Ephesians 5:31-32, God describes sex as a "profound mystery."
- Sex was a part of His original plan or else male and female bodies would not be different, and the entire human race would not be able to survive. However, sex was not intended solely for reproductive purposes; it comes with a deeper meaning, involving special love between two people (male and female)
- Sex was created for one, and only one institution: Marriage.
  - ➤ People try to blur the lines by making it seem like it's all right to have sex if they're *almost* married, or if they think they'll be getting married in the future. It is important that as Christian youths, we realize that

those labels are just excuses we make to engage in counterfeit intimacy.

- God's boundary (no sex before marriage) provides the best for us, and protects us from the worst.

Society's Idea of Sex

- Generally speaking, the media depicts sex as a cheap activity. They strip sex of its original purpose and portray it as a meaningless practice. The world encourages people to separate their bodies from their minds and emotions.
- As a matter of fact, teen magazines do promote sex, as long as the people engaging in it are protected in some way. Most issues of these magazines include topics about condoms and birth control pills.
  - ➤ The truth of the matter is that one out of every five-condom batches do not meet U.S. standards. Note that not every condom is tested for holes and they do break or slip off 15% of the time.
  - ➤ The intake/use of birth control pills has dangerous side effects such as headaches, weight gain, nausea, depression, blood clots, etc.

Consequences (Physical, Emotional, and Spiritual) of Sexual Activities

- ❖ **Physical Consequences:**

Pregnancy

- ➤ Pregnancy is the greatest fear associated with pre-marital sex Statistics show that more than 3,000 teen girls in the U.S. get pregnant everyday.
- ➤ Statistics also show that a teen father would actually end up paying between $50,000 and $250,000 depending on his income, until his child turns 18.
- ➤ Sadly, 9 out of 10 guys abandon their pregnant girlfriends.
- ➤ Pregnant teen girls are seven (7) times more likely to commit suicide than other girls of their age.
- ➤ 1/3 of teen moms drop out of high school, and half of them live at, or below the poverty level.

Pregnant youth must then face the options of keeping the baby, getting an abortion, or giving the baby up for adoption. Instead of celebrating pregnancies, they are regretting it because they failed to follow the word of God.

Sexually Transmitted Diseases (STDs)

➢ STDs are infections that are passed from one person to another during sexual activities. Some STDs are bacterial (they are treatable), while others are viral (there is no cure).

➢ Of the 12 million people in the U.S. infected with an STD, 3 million are teenagers.

➢ The most common bacterial STD is Chlamydia, which at times gives no symptoms. The most common viral STD is Human Papillomavirus (genital warts). There is also herpes, gonorrhea, syphilis, and HIV/AIDS. Lack of symptoms, does not imply absence of disease.

➢ Warts, early sex and multiple sex partners predispose females to cervical cancer.

Emotional Consequences

➢ Sexually active people outside wedlock must deal with emotional consequences such as guilt, depression, loneliness, rejection, worry, fear, regret, and anger.

➢ However, when a married couple engages in sex, there's no need to worry because they are involved in it within the institution meant for it by God

Spiritual Consequences –Soul Trouble

➢ There's an analogy that describes Christians as fish, and Satan as the fisherman. In order to catch the fish, Satan releases the right bait, which in this case is temptation. Temptations include TV programs, Internet pornographic sites, magazines, clothes that show too much skin, and the illusion of "safe sex." Satan lets down the bait into the water, and lures people into sin that way.

➢ The above analogy leads to separation from God and this translates to spiritual death.

➢ Sexual desire and being physically attracted to someone is not a sin. It's absolutely normal, and everyone experiences it. However, when we <u>focus</u> on that sexual desire that's when we sin. According to James, desire gives birth to sin, and sin gives birth to death. (James 1:14-15).

Question

What is our stand: Disease prevention or fear of God? Discuss.

Prayer

✓ Lord give me the grace to live above all forms of sexual sin.
✓ Lord, help me to recognize the bait of the enemy and to swim far away from it.

Conclusion

"Let us hear the conclusion of the whole matter: Fear God and keep his commandments for this is man's all. For God will bring every work into judgment, including every secret thing, whether good or evil." (Eccl.12:13-14).

Daily Bible Reading

1. The world is filled with corruption. (*Eph 2:2, 2 Peter 2:3-4*)
2. The world pollutes our minds. (*James 1:27, 1 John 2:15-17*)
3. If we are friends of the world, we are enemies of God. (*James 4:4, 1 John 2:15-17*)
4. On the other hand, everyone who sins is a slave to sin. (*John 8:32-36*)
5. Young men/ladies can cleanse their ways only by taking heed to God's word (*Ps. 119:9-16*)
6. God's grace is sufficient for us to live righteously (Titus 2:11-14).

31

YOUTH AND SEXUALITY
(PRACTICAL DISCUSSION)

Text: 1 Cor. 6:16-20

Memory Verse:
*"You were bought at a price; therefore glorify God
in your body and your spirit, which are God's"
(1 Cor. 6:20).*

Focus
- To have practical discussion among youth
- To show proper precautions youth can take in order to
  ensure that they do not fall into the trap of, or be
  exposed to the pressures of premarital sex.

Introduction
Masturbation (having sex with oneself) is <u>not</u> in the will of God.
Hebrews 13:4 states, *"Marriage is to be held in honor among all,
and the marriage bed is to be undefiled, for fornicators and
adulterers God will judge."* Self-stimulation defiles the marriage
bed. It also reduces the mystery of sex to a solo activity that
doesn't embrace the body, soul, and spirit.

Decisions...Decisions
- ➢ As Christian youths, we must make a decision whether
  to serve God, or physical pleasure. Romans 8:5 states,
  *"Those who live according to the sinful nature have
  their minds set on what that nature desires, but those
  who live in accordance with the Spirit have their minds
  set on what the Spirit desires."*
- ➢ The only way to have a fulfilling sexual relationship in
  the context of marriage is by practicing abstinence.
  Abstinence means no premarital sex.

- It is not always easy and we may experience ridicule, rejection, and frustration as a result of abstinence, but in the long run, the reward will be well worth it. Males may be referred to as impotent, females may be called frigid; but you know who you are.

- Jesus said that we should deny ourselves and follow him in all areas of our lives, including sexual activity. If we deny our flesh, we will be able to serve God wholeheartedly (2 Tim. 2:22).

- Abstinence is liberating. It provides freedom from the fear of pregnancy, the dangers of diseases, emotional pain, guilt, etc. (1 Cor. 9:27).

Note to the Male Youth: Sex is not a game. It's understandable that you all may have to face sexual struggles everyday, however, having sex does not make you a man. As a matter of fact, anyone can have sex, even animals, so it proves nothing with regards to your masculinity. Rather, having character, integrity and respect for women is what makes you a man. You must think beyond temporary pleasure. Pleasure of sin is but for a moment.

Note to the Female Youth: There is no need to rush, and the world will not cast you aside for not having sex. If you don't give in to your flesh, you will be known as someone who has character, integrity, depth, and self-control. Your temperance will show that you are not under the control of a sexual drive–you are much stronger than hormones, and you respect yourself and others. Waiting for sex won't kill you! Having premarital sex is not a proof of love or faithfulness to a relationship. Do not give in as a show of love.

Conclusion

Ephesians 5 describes sex as a "great mystery," which was created to be an enjoyable experience for married couples only. As youths, we must take proper precautions to ensure that we do not fall into the trap of, or be exposed to the pressures of premarital sex.

- We should try our best to date in groups to avoid tempting situations with members of the opposite sex.
- Run away from ALL tempting situations (avert your gaze, close the magazine, turn off the TV, etc) (2 Samuel 11-12).
- Don't indulge in fantasies = Do not let our minds dwell on sexual thoughts. (2 Samuel 13:1-11).
- Surround ourselves with people who will encourage and support our commitment to sexual purity (1 Cor. 15:33).
- And most importantly, we should commit our plans unto the Lord, and He will surely see us through. Proverbs 3:5-6 says *"Trust in the Lord with all your heart and lean not to your own understanding; in all your ways acknowledge him, and he will make your paths straight."* We should not exclude God from areas of our lives concerning sex. Rather, we must always trust God and believe within our hearts that His plan is best for us.

God did not create boundaries to restrict us from "living our lives." Instead, they were created to give us an opportunity to experience life abundance. Abstinence is both the wisest, and the safest choice.

Questions
1. If you have close friends who keep talking about their sexual experiences, what should you do?
2. What is God's stand homosexuality?
3. If you love someone deeply, and the person starts pressurizing you to have sex what should you do?
4. What role can parents play in helping their children prevent sexual immorality?

Prayer
Lord help me to stand my ground to abstain even in the face of opposition/worldly pressure
Lord help me to see far beyond the flimsy pleasures of today in order to enjoy tomorrow when I get married.

Daily Bible Readings

1. Sexual immorality and impurity are improper for God's people. *(Eph. 5:3-4).*
2. We should be sanctified and control our bodies in ways that are holy and honorable. *(1 Thessalonians 4:3-5).*
3. Do not offer parts of your body to sin. *(Romans 6: 11-13).*
4. God's truth gives us freedom to have real life. *(John 8:32, 34-36).*
5. Do not take God's forgiveness for granted. *(Romans 6:1).*
6. God doesn't tempt anyone. *(James 1:12-14)*

Reference:

Edmonton, H. "Youth, Sexuality and Abstinence." Times 10 Vol. 7 (1999): Nov 1999 <http://www.times10.org/cvr1199.htm>

ETR's Resource Center for Adolescent Pregnancy Prevention; Statistics. <http://www.etr.org/recapp/stats/>

Mueller, W. Understanding Today's Youth Culture. Illinois: Tyndale House Publishers, Inc., 1999.

Purpura, J. "Youth and Spiritual Direction."
        <http://www.antiochian.org/youth_spiritual_direction>
Stenzel, P. Sex Has a Price Tag: Discussions about Sexuality, Spirituality, and Self Respect. California: Youth Specialties Books, 2003.

NOTES

32

REBELLION AGAINST GOD

Text: 1 Samuel 15

Memory Verse:

"For rebellion is as the sin of witchcraft, and Stubbornness is as iniquity and idolatry. Because you have rejected the word of the Lord, He also has rejected you from being King"
(1 Sam. 15:23).

Focus

- To teach that rebellion is not of God
- To enumerate various ways in which people could rebel against God

Definition

Rebellion is an act of resistance to God and any institution that He puts in place. It is an act or a show of defiance toward an authority. To resist, revolt, rise up against, raise uprising, insurgency or opposition by force to an established authority is an act rebellion. To rebel against God is to act contrary, in deliberate disobedience, to His authority. Rebellion is a mutiny against God. It is a seditious act in deliberately disobedience to God's order. It is like teaming up against God to bring down His kingdom.

Introduction

Rebellion is not new; it has been in existence since time immemorial. The first rebel in the Bible was Lucifer the devil. As the Bible records, Lucifer was one of the Angels in heaven under the constituted authority of God. He occupied an exalted position of the lead singer in heaven until he rebelled against God (Rev. 12:7-9).

God is the creator of the universe. He rules by His sovereign power and authority. He created us with the intent that we may serve and worship Him. Anything (intent or action) contrary to the order of God is an act of rebellion. As a child of God, you cannot serve two masters. *(Matt. 6:24)*. You cannot give thought to, practice or imagine acts that are objectionable, detestable, abhorrent and offensive to God.

Actions That Could Lead To Rebellion:

As a creation of God, there are many ways in which a person could rebel against God. If any of the following is manifesting in one's life, one needs to amend his or her ways (Romans 12:2).

- **Association with unbeliever**: You cannot serve two masters. You cannot please God and the world. If you are a Christian and you still do everything your non-Christian neighbors are doing, this can lead into sin of rebellion. Examples are: Late night partying, credit card fraud, fornication, cohabitation before marriage, adultery, lying, etc (Luke 16:13, 2 Cor. 6:14, Gal. 5:19).

- **Disregard of The Great Commission**: A Christian without evangelism is a dead Christian. The first Apostles were called Christians in Antioch as a result of their Christ-like lifestyles. The command is clear and precise. "Go Ye...." If you are not witnessing, you are a rebel (Matt. 28:19-20).

- **Failure to pay tithe**: The Church represents the kingdom of God on earth, created by God. He put in place a solid structure to maintain and sustain her existence. Payment of tithe and offering is a command from God. If you are not paying, you are working against God, you are a rebel. **Malachi 3:8-12.**

- **Lack of Forgiving Spirit:** The Bible says "So My heavenly father also will do to you if each of you, from his heart, does not forgive his brother his trespass." **Matt. 18:35.** Unforgiving spirit is like cancer. It will damage both your spiritual and physical organs. If you harbor unforgiving

spirit, you are a rebel. **Matt. 18:21-35**. **Colossians 3:13.**
Failure to forgive others is an act of rebellion

- **Lackadaisical Approach to God's Business**: God's business is a serious business and it should be taken as such. Careless attendance in the Church is a clear sign of rebellion, even though one may not think of it (Heb. 10:25). Murmuring and complaints regarding any cause that will advance the work of God is a sign of lack of touch with God. **Acts 4:32, Acts 9:36-41.**

Conclusion

The greatest act of rebellion is rejecting the only acceptable sacrifice God Himself provided, the man Jesus Christ. Failure to surrender our heart to God in worship is rebellion. Rebellious spirit does not develop in one day; it is one thing that leads to another which eventually leads to an act of rebellion (Heb. 3:7-11).

Prayer:

✓ Help me Lord to live a life of obedience to your command.
✓ Help me to please you in all my undertakings.

Daily Bible Readings.

1. Man rebelled against God's instruction, hoping to be more wise (Genesis 3: 1-24).
2. The people rebelled against God by refusing to enter Canaan (Num. 14: 1-10).
3. God was ready to disinherit the people for their disobedience (Numbers 14: 11-25).
4. The rebels will die in the wilderness (Numbers 14:26-45).
5. The Israelites rebelled against God in not obeying His instructions (Ezek. 20: 18-24).
6. We are to take heed so we do not fall into the same sin of rebellion (Heb. 3:12-19).

33

REBELLION AGAINST AUTHORITY

Text: Numbers 12:1-13

Memory Verse:
"Let every soul be subject to the governing authorities. For there is no authority except from God, and the authorities that exist are appointed by God."
(Romans 13:1, NKJV)

Focus
- To enumerate various ways in which we could rebel against authority
- To elaborate on the consequences of rebellion
- To show the benefits of obedience

Introduction
People often put up acts of rebellion against human authorities, not knowing or pretending not to know that all acts of riot and disobedience is against God. They say, "You are not God, so I don't have to listen to you." On the contrary, God has called us to obedience (Titus 3:1).

Types of Authorities
- **The Government:** The government is the civil authority that rules over a State or community. This institution is recognized by God and He expects us to obey the rules and regulations set in place for the benefits of their subjects. 1 Peter 1:13. We however must know that every authority is subordinate to the authority of God (Acts 5:29).

- **The Church:** The Church is the body of Christ. It is the embodiment of God's presence on earth. Our Lord Jesus Christ created this institution and declared that no gate of hell shall prevail over the Church. Every step taken to frustrate the Church is a gate of hell. Matt 16:18.

  The Home: The role of the man, woman and the children are clearly stated. Each role player must be respected as we respect God. Anything contrary to this ordained order of God could be chaotic. If the man and the woman will play their God given roles, the peace of God will reign in the home. Eph. 5:21.

- **Institutional:** The leadership structure in your work place is a type of authority that must be respected and obeyed. Eph. 6: 5-8.

Traits of Rebellious Activities

Rebels are faultfinders. They are intolerable, resentful and are undependable. The spirit of rebellion could kill the joy of a family, mar the operation of the Holy Spirit in the Church, cause demotion or stagnation at work or set a nation on the path of destruction. Satan is the author of rebellion, sometimes his activities are subtle, at other times, they are obvious. The following are traits of rebellious activities:

1. **In Homes:** Marriage is an institution ordained by God. The leadership structure of our homes has been created by God at creation. Lack of submission, disrespect, and the likes are direct attacks of Satan on families. When you follow the order of God, the government of your home will run smoothly as intended by God. Try it. 1 Peter 3:1-8

2. **Confrontational Attitude Against Leadership:** Deliberate confrontation and disobedience to constituted authority is a major trait of rebellion. This could lead to pain, even death. Sheba rebelled against David. 2 Samuel 20:1 & 22.

3. **Usurping Authority**: When we usurp or hijack the role of a leader, it is a trait of rebellion. Even anyone who co-operates or takes pleasure in such activities will also be guilty of the same offense (Number 16:1-35). The wrath of God at His appointed time is the consequence of such act.

4. **Speaking Evil of Leaders**: You cannot drive the bus from the back. Cooperation with our leaders will advance the ministry of our Lord Jesus Christ. Rebellion is anti-progress. It gives birth to pain and death. Shimei rebel against David and earned destruction. 2 Samuel 16:5-8

Questions:

1. What are the other ways we exhibit rebellion in our home?
2. How can we exterminate the spirit of rebellion in our lives?

Conclusion

"Therefore, as the Holy Spirit says; today if you will hear His voice, do not harden your heart as in the rebellion, in the day of trial in the wilderness, where your fathers tested me, tried me and saw my works forty years. Therefore I was angry with that generation and said, they always go astray in their heart, and they have not known my ways. So I swore in my wrath, they shall not enter my rest." Hebrew 3:7-11.

Prayer:

✓ Help me Lord to live a life of obedience to your command.
✓ Remove high mindedness and pride from me, Oh Lord.

Daily Bible Readings.

1. Honor your master: 1 Tim. 6:1-10
2. Be sober-minded: Titus 2: 6-10
3. Submit to one another. Col.: 3: 18-25
4. Submit to Government. Rom. 13: 1-8
5. Submission at home. 1 Pet. 3:1-7
6. Pay your dues. Matt. 17:24-27, 1 Pet. 2: 13-17

34

MOCKING GOD & HIS MESSENGERS

Text: Hebrews 3:1-11

Memory Verse:

"But they mocked the messengers of God, despised His words, and scoffed at His prophets, until the Wrath of the Lord arose against His people, till there was no remedy"
(2 Chro. 36:16).

Focus

To elaborate on the consequences of rebellion

Introduction

In the secular world, rebellion is not without consequences. So is it in spiritual matters. However, it is rather unfortunate, that the consequences of rebellion in spiritual things often manifest physically. Many at times, Christians are not sensitive enough to link issues as "cause and effect". Instead of repenting from rebellious acts, we begin to look for physical solutions to spiritual judgments.

Consequences of Rebellion

- **Rejection**: God abhors rebellion. He is a God of mercy and justice with longsuffering. He rejects anyone that is rebellious against His command (Romans 1:18-26). Rebellion could take one from the throne to the pit. Adam and Eve were sent out from the place described as heaven on earth (paradise) to the wilderness to till the ground (Gen. 2:23). Saul the king out of rebellion the kingdom was taken away from him (1 Sam 15:23).

119

- **Curses**: Adam and Eve rebelled against God and they were cursed (Gen 3:14-24). Obedience leads to life while rebellion brews woes and pain. An act of rebellion could lead to the manifestation of curses and satanic influence in the life of a believer (Deut. 28:15-68).

- **Spiritual and physical death**: Rebellion could lead to spiritual and physical death. Rebellion sinks a believer to the point of sinning without remorse. The end result is spiritual deterioration and moral bankruptcy. The Israelites suffered physical death in captivity (Jeremiah 25:8-11).

- **Removal of God's shield and protection**: Deut.: 28:25, Judges 2:1-4. God commanded the Israelites not to co-mingle with the other nation so as not to get corrupted, but they did. God took away their protection. He said that those nations will be thorns and snares to them and that He will not drive the enemies out before them. If you rebel against God, the fruit of your rebellion may be the tool of your punishment (Num. 14:41-45).

- **Rebellion Leads to Spiritual Dryness/pain:** Any worker in the Church that is rebellious will be dry. It breaks the covenant. It results to suffering- Num 14. Israelites were made to wander in the wilderness, their 40 days was multiplied by 10years. Samson paid with spiritual dryness and death (Judges 16:20).

Question

1. Give current practical examples, where trouble came on people as a result of rebellion.
2. What role does rebellion play in present day tribal wars?

Prayer

✓ Every difficulty I have brought on myself by any rebellious act, forgive me oh Lord.

✓ Be merciful on me, and help me repair all damages done by my acts of rebellion.

Conclusion

Whatsoever a man sows, that will he reap. Rebellion caused Saul the throne. Korah died a shameful death. Miriam became leprous. Be careful, think through your actions before you embark on them. The worst of all is missing heaven after all your journey as a Christian. Repent, God in His mercy will forgive in Jesus name.

Daily Bible Reading

1. Rebellion of Zedekiah against God and Nebuchadnezzar brought prompt military siege on Jerusalem. Zedekiah lost his children, people and the throne (Jer. 52: 1- 11).
2. When the people of Judah refused to repent despite warnings from God, they were taken into captivity in Babylon (2 Chro. 36:15-21).
3. Repercussion of disobeying God (Deut. 28:15-35).
4. Non-productivity can result from disobedience (Deut., 28: 36-51).
5. Famine may be judgment of disobedience (Deut. 28:52-68).
6. Blessings follow those who obey God (Deut. 28: 1-14).

35

DO NOT ENVY SINNERS

Text: Psalms 37: 1-6

Memory Verse:
"Rest in the Lord and wait patiently for Him; Do not fret because of him who prospers in his ways, Because of the man who brings wicked schemes to pass." (Psalm 37:7, NKJV).

Focus:
- To understand the danger of envying the wicked.
- To learn how to prevent or overcome any form of envy.

Definition
Envy: Envy is a deep-seated ungodly desire to possess others' traits, accomplishments, abilities, material things etc. It is a discontent caused by another person's possession or achievement.

Introduction:
As in Malachi 3:13-15 - The way of the prosperous always appear right to others and it is assumed that he has to be doing something right for him to be so successful. However, a sinner may appear to have everything right, without any trouble: He works lazily yet gets a full pay. He is only good at eye service, but gets rewarded at promotion time. He is involved in shady business deals but makes unprecedented profit. She was so wayward as a single; she got the most comfortable man at a good age. He hardly does homework, cheats at examination hall, and gets a good grade and even scholarships! What more can we say about several sinners who have made it to the hall of fame, they have what it takes to be called successful by societal definition

of success. Even Asaph (a music minister appointed by David) had a period in his life when he envied the success of the wicked until he got better understanding of their end (Psalm 73: 1-3).

Why are people prone to envying the wicked?
They appear trouble free (Ps. 73:5, 12).
They seem self-sufficient (Ps. 73:7).
They speak loftily (Ps. 73:8).
They seem to get away with anti-God behaviors (Ps. 73:9, Job 21:14-15).
They are often powerful (Job 21:7).

What are the dangers in envying the ungodly?
It makes serving God appear to be in vain (Ps. 73: 13).

It makes trial of faith seem as plague (Ps. 73: 14a).

It makes correction in righteousness unfair punishment (Ps. 73: 14b).

It can lead to backsliding (Ps. 73:2).

What is the expected end of evildoers
Their ways are slippery (Ps. 73: 18).

They are brought to desolation suddenly (Ps. 73: 19).

They are easily blown away like straw (Job 21: 18).

They have no standing on the Day of Judgment (Ps. 1:5).

How to prevent envying the ungodly
Have a good understanding of their end, so that you do not envy their present (Ps. 37:9).

Know that God does not forsake his saints, so no matter the situation now, God will make a way (Ps. 37:28).

Remember that the righteous will in the long run inherit the earth (Ps. 37: 29).

Keep God's law in your heart, so that your feet will be grounded (Ps. 37: 30-31).

Questions

1. Mention other things that tempt Christians to envy sinners.
2. Give practical examples of some mighty people who have fallen suddenly.
3. Give any personal experience where like Asaph you felt like the wicked are excelling and at a point you thought whether serving God was worth the effort.
4. Fill in the gap: As for me, my feet was almost ---------, my steps had near ---------. For I was ----------at the foolish, when I ------------- the ------------- of the wicked (Ps. 73:2-3).

Conclusion

It takes the grace of God to be sustained through thick and thin when you see those who do not profess God prospering. If one does not quickly come to the realization of the end of the wicked like Asaph did it is easy to loose the salvation of the soul. The sinner has another opportunity to repent today, as we realize that the end is destruction. Christ came to save the entire world from this destruction, including the worst sinner. Why not repent today and accept Jesus Christ as Lord and savior.

Daily Bible Reading

1. Do not desire to keep the company of evil men (Pro. 24:1-2)
2. Blessed is the man that does not walk in the counsel of the ungodly (Ps. 1:1-6)
3. The fear of the Lord brings blessing and contentment (Ps. 128:1-2).
4. Envy is the mother of all kinds of sin (2 Sam.11:1-15).
5. Envy brings punishment (2 Sam. 12:1-14).
6. Do not envy sinners, because there is a hereafter (Pro. 23: 4-18).

NOTES

36

SOUL WINNING: MY PERSONAL RESPONSIBILITY

Text: 1 Corinthians 9:16-17

Memory Verse:
"For if I preach the gospel, I have nothing to boast of, for necessity is laid upon me, yes, woe is upon me if I do not preach the gospel!"
(1 Cor. 9:16).

Focus:
To learn that soul winning is an individual responsibility and that there are consequences for disobedience to the command regarding evangelism.

Introduction:
Jesus has called everyone individually to the task of soul winning and each Christian must take this responsibility serious. When Jesus gave the instruction in Mk.16:15, saying "go into all the world…" He was commissioning each of us. Soul winning means evangelizing sinners, winning and bringing them to Christ for salvation, sanctification and service in God's house.

Basis of Individual Responsibility in Soul Winning:
- Jesus individually invited His disciples to take their cross and follow him (Mt. 9:9).
- Jesus called Peter to feed His sheep/flock (Jn. 21:15,17)
- Jesus himself took the task of soul winning personal, called it His father's business and took the responsibility of personally advancing it. (Luke 2:49 & John 9:4).

According to Matt. 25:19-30 there is either a reward for obedience and punishment for neglect of this important duty.

Rewards for fulfilling the great commission:
- Soul winners' labors will not be in vain (Heb. 6:10)
- Those who worked well will come with joy to give their reports (Matt.25: 20) and they will receive crowns of life.
- They shall shine as stars forever in God's kingdom (Dan 12:3; Matt. 13:43).

Punishment for neglecting the great commission:
- Those who did not work will give excuses but only to land them in hell (Matt. 25:24-30).
- Anyone who neglects this duty will be beaten with many stripes and be sentenced to hell for disobedience. (Luke 12:47-48)

Question
How can we effectively do personal evangelism in our various community?

Conclusion
It is reassuring to know that God sees everything we do for Him, especially in the area of evangelism and that He will reward all for their services. Today many Christians wish to experience miracles in their lives as in the time of the Apostles, however they do not preach the gospel as the apostles did. We must know that the promises are for those who go out and preach. We must see ourselves as individually responsible for the lives of others and we must never be ashamed of preaching the gospel.

Daily Bible Reading:
1. Preaching the gospel is a responsibility –Matt 25:14-18.
2. You need dedication and separation to preach the gospel – Mark 1:16-20.
3. Successfully discipling others need prayers –Luke 6:12-16.
4. Sign will follow if you preach the gospel –Mark 16:15-18.
5. Paul had established a custom of preaching and teaching where ever he went (Acts 17: 1-4).
6. We shall report our services to the Master Jesus one of these days (Matt. 25:14-19)

127

37

RESPONSIBILITY OF SOUL-WINNERS TO THEIR COMMUNITIES

Text: 1 Corinthians 9:16-23

Memory Verse:

"Take heed to yourself and to the doctrine.
Continue in them, for in this you will save both
yourself and those who hear you"
(1 Timothy 4:16, NKJV).

Focus:

To learn the responsibility of soul winners to the community.

Introduction:

Success is not actualized until others benefit from it; therefore merely knowing Christ is not enough. Hence we must win other souls for Christ in other for us to be considered successful in God's sight.

In order to achieve the goal of soul winning, one is responsible to:

1. **Be Transparent**
   - Live a life that attracts people to Christ (1 Cor. 9:19-23).
   - Maintain good conduct and be an example unto others as Jesus teaches (Matt. 5:14-16)

2. **Meet Community Needs**   (John 4:4-30)
   - Identify the needs in your community and provide for such needs as much as lies within your power. As you meet their needs, you get their attention and are able to speak life and liberation to them. Jesus seizes an opportunity of the need of the woman at the well to give her life. Jesus went about doing good (Jn. 2:1-8).

Give the message of reconciliation not condemnation (John 3:17)

- Christ came to restore sinners to original position with God (John 10:10)
- Present a loving Savior, willing to accept people just as they are (Matt 9: 12)
- From the state they are, Christ is able and willing to move them forward (Luke 4:18-19)
- Give them hope for a more guaranteed future (Jn 14:1-4)

How the Gospel should be preached in our Community:
It must be preached ...
- In obedience (Mark 16:15-20)
- In faith (Hebrews 11:6) and love (John 1:45-49)
- With expectancy (Acts 10:34-38) and urgency (Lk. 1:15-18)

Conclusion:

Looking at the whole ministry of Jesus Christ, we notice that he went about doing good. It is therefore important to conclude that being transparent with people, meeting them at points of needs and preaching the message of Christ's reconciliation will open doors to evangelize people's hearts.

Questions:

How many times should I preach the Gospel in a week?

Prayer

Father, please make me a fisher of men to your glory in Jesus name.

Daily Bible Reading

1. Talk to others about preaching Christ (John 1:43-46).
2. Preaching is a requirement (1 Corinthians 9:16-17).
3. We are the bearers of the Light of the Gospel (Matt. 5:13-16).
4. To do this is to receive a reward (Daniel 12:3, James 5:19).
5. Teach by example (1 Timothy 4:11-14).
6. Pressing toward the goal. (Philippians 3:10-15).

38

FELLOWSHIP
(EXPERIENCING LIFE TOGETHER)

Text: Psalm 133:1

Memory Verse
"God is faithful, by whom you were called into the fellowship of His Son, Jesus Christ our Lord"
(1 Cor. 1:9, NKJV).

Focus
To learn and understand how to "fellowship" – God's way.

Introduction
In most cases we understand fellowship to mean socialization, eating and having fun or attending church. No wonder we sometimes say, "Where do you fellowship?" "Stay for fellowship after church," etc. But this study will reveal fellowship in a deeper and different light. When the Bible speaks of fellowship, it means "having joint interest," "sharing," and "experiencing life together." Therefore we want to learn how to experience life together with Christ and fellow Christian.

There are two types of fellowship in God's family:
1. Fellowship with God (1 John 1:3 & 2 Cor. 13:14)
- ✓ Having joint interests with God, i.e., receiving God's love and giving Him ours in return (Rm. 8:3-39).
- ✓ Sharing God's holy character and nature (1 Jn. 2:6). This means we share His views and interests about life. God's view of life is: (a) loving our brethren [1 Jn. 2:9-11]; (b) refraining from loving the lusts of this world [1 Jn. 2:15-17]; (c) abiding in His words [1 Jn. 2: 24-29].
- ✓ When we enjoy His presence (Ps. 4:6).

130

2. **Fellowship with one another as brethren (1 John 1:7)**
   a) In godly fellowship we **share honesty**. People become honest with each other about what is happening in their own lives. People share their hurts, failures, feelings and doubts.
      - We admit our fears, acknowledge our weaknesses and ask for help and prayers.
      - We are able to confess our sins one to another (James 5:16; 1 John. 1:7-8).
      - When we share honesty, we do not put up guards, wear masks or act as if everything is rosy.
      - Admittedly that this type of life is risky and requires humility and courage, but this is the only way we can grow.

   b) In godly fellowship **people experience giving and receiving.** This involves reciprocity, mutuality, responsibility sharing, helping one another and becoming encouraged together in mutual faith (Rm. 1:12).

   c) In godly fellowship **we practice hospitality (Rm. 12:13).** This means loving strangers. Christ's instruction in **Mk. 6:8** assumes hospitality; the disciples could even have choices of where they stayed **(Mt. 10:11)** and they could stay as long as they wanted **(Lk. 10:7).** Jesus finishes it by saying if we give an ordinary cup of water to preacher or anyone because of Him, we will receive rewards **(Mt. 10:42).**

   d) In godly fellowship **people experience sympathy with each other (Gal. 6:1-2).** On page 141 of "Purpose Driven Life," Rick Warren says sympathy is entering in and sharing the pain of others, not just offering quick answers or giving cosmetic advice to people. Each time we understand and affirm someone's feelings, we build fellowship." Even when our situations are so tough and it seems as if God is distanced, we need fellowship (sharing) to help reaffirm to each other that there is still a God in heaven who cares.

e) In godly fellowship **mercy wins over judgment** (James 2:13). We need to offer to and receive mercy from each other. Since God has forgiven us we must forgive others because there cannot be fellowship without forgiveness. Yes, it takes a great deal of mercy to sustain fellowship. We must learn to make allowance for each other's faults and then forgive **(Col. 3:13).**

Question
People are difficult to deal with. What would make it easy to have true fellowship?

Conclusion
Because with God all things are possible, one can depend on His faithfulness to help one maintain joint interests with Him and our fellows. Our love for each other will reflect our love for Christ and it our fellowship with Christ will reflect on our fellowship with people.

Prayer Point
✓ Lord grant me the grace for true fellowship with you and my brethren.

Daily Reading
1. Walking like Jesus (1 John 2:1-end)
2. Fellowship with Jesus is necessary for growth (John 15:1-8)
3. When we suffer for Christ's sake (Rom 15:1-2; Rom 12:15)
4. Loving each other (John 15:9-17)
5. Partaking of the Lord's Supper is fellowshipping (1 Cor.11:24-25).
6. Bring unbelievers to fellowship with Christ (Matt. 28:16-20).

References
Easton's Bible Dictionary; "Purpose Driven Life" by Rick Warren; New Unger's Bible Dictionary.

39

THE RAPTURE
(As An Event of His Second Coming)

TEXT: 1 Thess. 4:13-18

Memory Verse:

"Behold, I tell you a mystery: We shall not all sleep, but we shall all be changed — in a moment, in the twinkling of an eye, at the last trumpet. For the trumpet will sound, and the dead will be raised incorruptible, and we shall be changed."
(1 Cor. 15:51-52, NKJV)

Focus

To understand the event and process of the rapture

What is Rapture?

The English word "rapture" is derived from the Latin verb meaning 'caught up.' So rapture is the sudden 'catching up' of believers into heaven when Christ "descends from heaven with a shout, with the voice of an archangel, and with the trumpet of God" (1 Thess. 4:13-18).

This catching up will involve both the 'dead in Christ' and 'the living in Christ.' 1 Thess: 4:16-17 affirms that the dead in Christ will rise first, then those who are alive in Christ will be caught up with them in the clouds to meet the Lord.

Here the Apostle Paul described the hope that awaits Christians both who have died and those who are still alive. He assures them that there is resurrection: a process of putting death to shame and receiving a glorious body which reigns with Christ forever. Paul felt the importance of explaining issues to the people in Corinth, Thessalonica, as well the church of today so that we will know the truth on the subject and avoid unnecessary sorrow about the condition of our future.

The death of saints is always referred to as falling asleep (John 11:11; 1 Cor 11:30; 15:51). Paul maintains that there is hope; therefore, we should not sorrow as the unbelievers do. In fact, resurrection is the advantage we have over those who are not Christians. Glory Halleluiah. The process of this glorious resurrection (both for the dead and the living in Christ) is what we call 'rapture' (1 Thess. 4:14; 1 Cor. 15:12-14). This is the process which will fulfill Jesus' assertion in John 14:3 saying, *"And I go and prepare a place for you, I will come again and receive you to Myself; that where I am, there you will be also." (NKJV)*

Resurrection is a miracle; we will experience this miracle on this glorious day that we are talking about *(1 Thessalonians 4:15)*.

The Process:

Rapture follows a process. It is not going to happen in an unordered/disorganized manner (1 Thess. 4:16-17).

First, the Lord himself shall descend from heaven with a shout, with the voice of the archangel, and with the trump of God:
Secondly, the dead in Christ shall rise
Thirdly, those of us who are yet to die will be caught up together with them (the dead in Christ who have just risen) in the clouds to meet the Lord in the air.

The Event:

All of a sudden we will just hear **a shout** (a "cry' of excitement) coming with Christ in the clouds with a multitude who would lift up loud voice like that of an army rushing to a battle.

During the shout of trumpet announcing Christ's appearance, the world will just find out that some people are missing. This is one day that you and I should be missing. If we are missing, it means we have been caught up with the Lord. But if you are the one who notices that somebody is missing, it means you have been left behind. Matt. 24:40-41which says, *"Then two men will be in the field: one will be taken and the other left. Two women will be grinding at the mill: one will be taken and the other left. (NKJV)*

The voice of the archangel and the trumpet make the announcement of the arrival of the Lord and summon the world to the bar of judgment, so will the shout of Jesus (the Son of Man) be heard by those who are in the graves and they will begin to rise (John 5:27-29).

Now once the sound is made, the 'dead in Christ,' i.e., Christians who had died before that time shall rise first (1 Thessalonians 4:17).

Before we are caught up, we too will go through a quick moment of death and resurrection (1 Cor 15:51-55). This is going to be an awesome experience. May we be counted worthy in Jesus name.

Once our bodies have been transformed from mortality to immortality, then all of us shall be caught up to meet our Lord in the sky. This is rapture. Now we do not need to worry about the force that will make us become caught up. The force and the power of the Holy Spirit which caught Philip away in Acts 8:39 will be made available to us. Ascending will not be done by our own controllable power but by the supernatural Spirit of God. This is why we need to possess the Holy Spirit now – since He is the force and power that will rapture (catch) us up. Witchcraft power, force or wings will not work that day.

Caught Up Where?
Into the clouds to meet the Lord in the air. We are going to be in the regions of the atmosphere-above the earth. Christ will be there and we will ascend to meet Him. Although the world has experienced many events that brought shock to it in different magnitudes, rapture will be the biggest of all. It will concern everybody on the face of the earth. Rapture will not be an event affecting only a few countries or people.

When will rapture take place?
No one knows precisely when this event will take place. The Bible warns us in 1 Thess. 5:2 however that it will be like a thief in the night (a surprise). It will be a sudden and fast event – 1 Cor. 15:52 says, "in a moment, in the twinkling of an eye …" Unlike non-Christians for whom rapture would sound scary and negative, joy and excitement will fill the hearts of Christians

when we talk about rapture. It is the time of glorification; a time of fellowshipping with the Lord and our loved ones who had left us before; it is a time of everlasting peace.

When we are busy focusing upon the rest and peace with Christ, the world will be left with chaos of the traffic accidents that took place when the Christian drivers of vehicles suddenly were caught up and car are left to crash. Planes will crash if the pilots are Christians; numerous passengers won't get back home because they would have been caught up etc.

Advantages of Being Rapture Ready
1. We will get to be like Jesus and see Him as He is (1 Jn. 3:2).
2. You will begin everlasting enjoyment (Rev. 21:4).
3. We won't have to suffer through the tribulation. (Lk. 21:36).

Questions
It is possible to have been a Christian and still miss the rapture; explain.

Conclusion
Be Ready. Accept Jesus Christ as your personal Lord and Savior. He that will come will soon come and He will not tarry (Matt 24:34-35).

Daily Bible Reading
1. Christ is risen, so our faith is not in vain (Cor. 15:12-58)
2. Do not sorrow for the dead, they are only sleeping (1 Thess. 4:13-14).
3. God hath not appointed us to wrath, but to obtain salvation by Jesus Christ (1 Thessalonians 5:9-10).
4. God will keep thee from the hour of temptation (Revelation 3:10).
5. There will be wars and rumors of wars towards the end of time (Matt. 24:1-8).
6. Wise people will be ready for this day (Matt. 25:1-13).

NOTES

40

CONTENTMENT

Text: Philippians 4:11-13.

Memory Verse:

"Not that I speak in regard to need, for I have learned in whatever state I am, to be content"
(Philippians 4:11)

Focus

- To teach the benefits of contentment.
- To teach on consequences of lack of contentment.

Introduction

To be content is to have an inner attitude of satisfaction with who you are and what you have. This inward satisfaction will reflect on our way of life and our disposition to things. Paul learnt to be contented in whatever state he was. His disposition was not based on availability of supplies. His source of motivation was not his ability to meet all needs at a point in time, but the knowledge of Christ who is able to sustain in all things. Hence he concluded that with the assurance of Christ he could do all things, irrespective of the present circumstance.

How can we be content?
Seek the giver not the gift: Paul enjoins Timothy to pursue righteousness. Your pursuit as a child of God ought not be what you can derive from serving God but a relationship with him. No one is interested in people who just associate with them because of the benefit derived instead of true love. If you stick to the giver more gifts are imminent (Matt. 6:33-34).

Recognize that everything acquired is only for a limited time:
We brought nothing into the world; certainly we are going with

nothing. Whatever material things we acquire whether skills, money, etc. are for the limited time we have here on earth (Job 1:21, Eccl. 5:15-16).

Differentiate between need and want: When we qualify every want as a need, there will be no satisfaction with what we have. Attempting to meet every want will result in an endless pursuit of material things. Your lifestyle should not be dictated by people, latest fashion, crave for designer wears etc.

Do not make money the goal for your existence (1 Tim. 6: 9-10)
Paul enjoined Timothy that people who live for riches will ensnare their souls. Money does not have the ability to change people; it only finds expression in the real person when available. Poverty does not glorify God (Pro.3: 8-9). In the same token, making money the goal for living will make it impossible for people to be satisfied with whatever they have (Pro. 23:4-5).

Benefits of Contentment
- It brings peace. One is not under pressure to be like someone else.
- It encourages gratitude for whatever is received (1 Tim. 1:12-13).
- It eliminates inferiority complex (2 Tim. 1:12).
- It saves from the sin of:
  1. Covetousness
  2. Acquiring things through unlawful means
  3. Envy and jealousy

Contentment does not equal Complacency
Paul though he learnt to be abased or full, he struggled for masteries in everything he did. He labored more than the other apostles and ensured completion of his goals (1 Cor. 9:26, 15:9-11). While we appreciate God for what He has helped us to achieve, we work at attaining greatness.

Questions

1. How do we free ourselves from the pressure of keeping up with current things?
2. How can we help people to differentiate between need and want?

Conclusion

The giver has more than you can ever request from Him. Instead of pursuing the gift why don't you pursue the giver so you can have a perpetual flow. The best you can give the giver is your soul. When you surrender yourself to him, and seek him all other things will be added to you (Matt.6: 33). Having food and basic needs, let us be content (1 Tim. 6:8).

Daily Bible Reading

1. All labors are in vain except God is in it (Ps. 127:1-5).
2. Our confidence should not be in the flesh (Phil. 3:1-11).
3. Self-discipline is essential in running the Christian race (1 Cor. 9:24-26).
4. When you fear God you will be happy and it shall be well with you (Ps.128: 1-6).
5. No matter what you have, if you do not have the power to enjoy it; all is vanity (Eccl. 6:1-11).
6. All we acquire is going to be left for others someday (Eccl. 2:17-23).

References
The Great Investment by T. D. Jakes

41

HINDRANCES TO CONTENTMENT
Text: 1 Timothy 6:6-10.

Memory Verse:
"And having food and clothing, with these we shall be content."
(1 Tim. 6:8, NKJV)

Focus
- To learn that contentment is a virtue.
- To understand the reasons for lack of contentment.

Definition
Contentment is a state of being satisfied or happy with what one is or has. This is the state where one says, "I have enough," "what I have is good for me," "I am okay with what I have."

Introduction
Amazingly, in Gen. 33:9,11, we see two brothers who both confidently said "I have enough." Although they had different characters and trades, spent most of their lives in different places, yet they were content. If you take time to look at the beginning of their lives, it may be fair to say Esau and Jacob were the least expected people to be content; yet we see them displaying contentment here.

Everyone has a motivating drive for life. This drive varies from one individual to another. It therefore, affects one's value for God, things, people and work. Some people are driven by the desire to be everything except what they presently are, resulting in lack of contentment with self. Some others are driven by materialism, thus all they live for is the quest to acquire more than they have at any point in time, at whatever cost. The desire for what they do not have outweighs the joy of all they have; hence they are also not contented.

Some reasons for lack of contentment

1. **When we allow material possession to determine our worth:** "your vales are not determined by your valuables". (R. Warren). "Self worth" and "net worth" are also not equal. More importantly, the things we attach great importance to are not necessarily what God values the most (Ps. 37: 16-17). Hence, God places more value on the righteousness of someone more than the riches of the person (Pro. 15:16). When we realize that our valuables do not translate to self worth, then we should take pleasure in what we have.

2. **When we allow positional power to determine our self worth:** many are disgruntled with their positions at work, home, community and even church, because they equate title to self worth. This has led to endless struggle for recognition, which has ravaged many organizations. Jesus made it clear that position should be for service and not for pride. (Matt. 20:25-28).

3. **When we practice religion instead of having relationship with God:** Many under this misconception have become moralist, practicing mere religion instead of seeking God. Service to humanity is good, but it should not replace our relationship with God. Such was the zeal that Saul had before he finally met Christ (Acts 26:4-5, 9-11). True contentment will come as we develop deeper relationship with God in our service to people and not in self-righteousness (Rom. 10: 1-4).

4. **When we have insatiable appetite/covetousness:** Jezebel went as far as committing murder all in an effort to acquire Naboth's vineyard for her husband (1 Kings 21:4-7). Here, the king wanted the land that belongs to

someone else, despite that he had access to the whole land of Israel. The Bible says "...for a man's life consists not in the abundance of the things which he possesses" (Luke 12:15). Let us know that every addition in material gain is also additional opportunity to serve. This is God's pleasure.

5. **Misunderstanding of God's purpose for creation:** "The purpose of your life is far greater than your own personal fulfillment, your peace of mind, or even your happiness. It's far greater than your family, your career, or even your wildest dreams and ambitions. If you want to know why you were placed on this planet, you must begin with God. You were born *by* his purpose and *for* his purpose" (Rick Warren). When we fail to recognize we are created to fulfill God's pleasure then we will not be contented with where God places us (Rev. 4:11).

6. **Impatience:** Every sown seed requires time to germinate and grow before producing fruit. In the present day, everyone including Christians are in a hurry to accomplish something. There is increasing impatience at experiencing the fulfillment of the promises of God that we become dissatisfied with the level we presently have attained (Ps. 37:7).

"If you strive to lay hold on something before you're due, you will be doomed." - David Oyedepo

---

Questions
1. What are other reasons why you think people are not contented?
2. What are some examples of people in the Bible that did not seem to be contented with what they had or whom they were?

Conclusion

The reason for your not been contented is not found in what you do or have; it is a matter of who you are. Your value is far above your material possession or your attained position. The kingdom of God is of more value than any thing we can possess. It is time to start appreciating God for what you have and who you are. What does it profit a man if he gains the whole world but lose his soul?

Prayer

✓ Forgive me Lord in all areas where I have been dissatisfied with who I am.
✓ Let me see your glory in all that you have helped me to achieve.

Daily Bible Reading

1. Deliberately set your mind on things above (Col. 3:1-10).
2. Jezebel died a shameful death for the murder of Naboth (2 Kings 9:30-37).
3. Do not envy workers of iniquity (Ps. 37:1-11).
4. All material possessions will someday become useless (Ps.49: 26-20).
5. No matter what you have, without contentment you cannot be satisfied (Eccl. 5:10-17).
6. Ability to enjoy the fruit of one's labor is the gift of God (Eccl. 5:18-20).

References
The Purpose Driven Life by Rick Warren
Understanding Financial Prosperity by David Oyedepo

42

RECOGNIZING GOD'S VOICE

Text: 1 Samuel 3:1-10

Memory Verse:

"My sheep hear My voice, and I know them, and they follow Me."
(John 10:27).

Focus:

- To know that God is still speaking today
- To learn the ways God speaks
- To learn how to recognize His voice in order to answer him

Introduction:

It is worth knowing that the Almighty God we serve is speaking even though we cannot see Him with our natural eyes. And he speaks in different ways today than He did with the people of the biblical times (Heb. 1:1-2). All we need to do is to be willing to hear from Him and to be ready to do what He says.

Class Participation

1. How do I know God is still speaking?
2. How do I recognize the voice of God?
3. How can I hear from God on a daily basis?

What Does the Bible teach?

- **Ways God Speaks**

God speaks through His Son, Jesus Christ (Heb. 1:1-2). Jesus said in John 10 that the sheep hears my voice. He is speaking to us everyday, but like sheep we must be close to the shepherd to hear his voice clearly. He expects us to hear his voice. The more we know Him the more he speaks to us. He speaks to encourage us, remove fear, give us direction, and edify us.

God Speaks to us through His words. The word is the medium of communication (1 Cor. 2:13 & Acts 8:26-35).

How Do You Hear Him?
Through meditation in the word. Revelation occurs during the quiet moments of meditation (Dan. 9:1-4). When you receive a revelation as you are reading the word, this is a clear sign that God is speaking to you. We can also hear God through meditative prayers whereby we ask God to speak to us in our quiet moments (Acts 10:1-3). We also hear Him directly through Holy Spirit's voice which can come to us anytime as long as we are fully surrendered to Him and living holy.

Results of Hearing Him
Hearing from God assures that we belong to Him (John 10:27)
It builds our spiritual lives (Ps. 119:50)
It makes our faith a reality, not just an abstract conviction. We become transformed (Col. 3:16).

Questions
Give Bible examples of people who heard from God and it delivered them from impending trouble.
Do you require a prophet all the time before you can hear from God?

Conclusion:
There is nothing to compare with hearing from God-the Almighty who has the Manual of our lives in His hands. If we are patient enough to hear from him each day, wrong steps will be far from us. Let us therefore allocate the good part of our hearts to hearing from Him.

Daily Bible Reading
1. Pray for ears that can hear God's voice (Pro. 20:11-12)

2. Hearing from God develops one's faith (Rom. 10:17-18)
3. We must be doers of His Word always, in order to make Him speak to us continually (Ezek. 33:30-33)
4. If we cultivate an act of hearing from God, we will not follow strangers (John 10:1-5)
5. Boldness-an instrument in hearing from God-(Ex. 20:18-21)
6. If we love Him, we will not fear hearing His voice (Deut. 5:27-31)

43

HOW TO RECOGNIZE GOD'S VOICE
Text: 1 Sam. 3:1-10

Memory verse:
"...And Samuel answered, 'Speak, for Your servant hears.'"
(1 Sam. 3:10, NKJV).

Fill in the blank with answers. Use the passages sited as a guide.

WHY IS IT IMPORTANT TO HEAR GOD?

1. **IT PROVES** _____
   Jesus: *"My sheep <u>recognize my voice</u> and follow me." John. 10:27 (NLT)*

2. **IT PROTECTS** _____
   "Listen for God's voice in everything you do, and everywhere you go; he's the one who will keep you on track." Pr. 3:6 (Msg)

3. **IT PRODUCES** _____
   "I will guide you along the <u>best pathway for your life</u>. I will advise you and watch over you." Ps. 32:8 (NLT)

PREPARING TO HEAR GOD SPEAK

Parable of the Soils -Luke 8:4-15

1. **CULTIVATE** _____
   "A farmer went out to sow his seed. As he was scattering the seed, <u>some fell along the path</u>; it was trampled on, and the birds of the air ate it up." Luke 8:5 (NIV)

"Those along the footpath are the ones who hear, and then the devil comes along and takes away the word from their hearts, so they cannot believe and be saved." Luke 8:12 (NIV)

The hardened soil = _____

3 Causes

•_____•_____•_____

"Get rid of all the filth and evil in your lives, and humbly accept the message God has planted in your hearts, for it is strong enough to save your soul." James 1:21 (NLT)

2. ALLOCATE _____
"Other seed fell on shallow soil with underlying rock. This seed began to grow, but soon it withered and died for lack of moisture." Luke 8:6 (NLT)

"The rocky soil represents those who hear the message with joy. But like young plants in such soil, their roots don't go very deep. They believe for a while, but they wilt when the hot winds of testing blow." Luke 8:13 (NLT)

The shallow soil = _____

"Don't give up the habit of meeting together; Instead, let us encourage one another." Heb. 10:25 (TEV)

3. ELIMINATE _____
"Other seed fell in the weeds; the weeds grew with it and strangled it." Luke 8:7 (Msg)

"The seed that fell among weeds stands for those who hear, but as they go on their way, they are choked by life's worries, riches, and pleasures, and they don't mature." Luke 8:14 (NIV)

The soil with weeds = _____

"...there was the sound of a <u>gentle whisper</u>." 1 Kings 19:12 (NLT)

4. COOPERATE _____
   "The seeds that fell in good soil stand for those who <u>hear </u>the message and <u>retain </u>it in a good and <u>obedient </u>heart, and they <u>persist</u> until they <u>bear fruit</u>." Luke 8:15 (GN)

The good soil = _____

"...They <u>listen</u> to God's words and <u>cling to them</u> and steadily <u>spread them to others</u> who also soon believe." Luke 8:15 (LB)

Note: anwers in the appendix

Daily Bible Reading

1. Samuel's heart was right before God, so he heard God even as a child (1 sam. 3: 2-14).
2. God speaks to through His word (2 Tim. 3:16-17).
3. God can speak through revelation (Ezek. 37: 1-14).
4. Man may not perceive God speaking if we are not sensitive to Him (Job 33: 14-15).
5. When we listen to God, He can give us directions on how to lead our life (Gen. 12:1-3).
6. God has in these last days spoken to us through His son (Heb. 1:1-2).

SANCTIFICATION

Text: Ephesians 5:25-27

Memory Verse:
"Sanctify them through thy truth thy word is truth"
(John 17:17)

Focus
To understand sanctification, its process, necessity and reward.

What is Sanctification
Simply put sanctification is seperation from the worldly way into God's way of doing things. It is leaving one lifeslyle for another. Sanctify in Greek terms means to "set apart" for God's use. This can can apply to persons, place, things, and special occasions:

- Aaron's descendants were consecrated as priests to offer sacrifice to God (Lev. 21:1, 8).
- Paul and Barnabas were seperated for God's work (Acts 13:2).
- The Isrealites were requested to sanctify themselves before crossing river Jordan (Jos.3:5).
- The Sabbath is holy unto God (Lev. 23:3) and it is lawful to do good on the sabbath (Matt 12: 12).

WHAT SANCTIFICATION IS NOT
Luke 11:24 teaches that one cannot afford just to move into the middle (in-between) but totally leave the devil's camp and move into God's camp. Therefore sanctification is not outward holiness, abstaining from marriage or certain kinds of food (1 Tim. 4:1-5). One must be transformed in the inner man.

Christains are set apart for God's use
At salvation we believe with our hearts and confess with the mouth the lordship of Jesus Christ (Rom. 10: 8-10). This

experience makes one born again and sets one apart from worldly things for the master's use. We are sanctified in Jesus and called to be saints (1 Cor.1:2). This seperation was by election according to God's foreknowledge by the offering of the body of Christ (Heb. 10:10, 2 Thess. 2:13, 1 Peter 1:2). Under the Mosiac ordinances, seperation was by repeated offering of sacrifices, but Christ is the perfect sacrifice offered once and for all, that gives us opportunity to be counted worthy of being seperated unto God for holy use.

WHY DO I NEED TO BE SANCTIFIED?
- In order not to grieve the Holy Spirit (Isa. 63:10 & Eph. 4:30).
- In order to walk with God (Amos 3:3)
- It is a command from God (Lev. 20:7)
- I have been set apart for God's work
- It is the will of God (1 Thess. 4:3)
- I'll be rewarded (Heb. 11:6)
- So that I can co-own what God owns (Gal. 4:7)

WHAT ARE THE RESULTS OF A SANCTIFIED LIFE?
- There will be a free flow of revelation and operation of the gifts of the Holy Spirit
- There will be quick answers to my prayers (Isa. 65:24)
- I will be able to do all things through Christ's strength.
- It will prevent backsliding (Ezra 9:1).

WHAT CAN I DO TO BE SANCTIFIED?
- Ask God in prayer to give you the grace for sanctification (1 Tim. 4:5)
- Examine yourself in the mirror of the Word of God (James 1:23-35); it is the WORD that sanctifies (John 17:17).
- Take decisive actions to eliminate everything that does not belong (2 Thess. 5:22; Eph. 4:22-24; Job 31:1)

- Replace every wrong with the right thir
  you through the spiritual heart surg̩
  (Ezek. 36)
- Rely upon the help of the Holy Spirit
  5:16).
- Continue to fellowship with brethren aₙₗₗ
  light. The blood of Jesus will continue the cleansing uₙₗₗ
  the coming of the Lord (1John 1:7).
- Put on the whole armor of God (Eph. 6:10)

Question

How does salvation differ from sanctification?
Can sanctification be realistic when we have to live every da
with unbelieving relations?

Conclusion

Although sanctification is a continuous process, you do not neͤ
the blood of bulls and rams. Just continue practicing the word
God which has the ability to renew your mind and the nature
sin will gradually erode and nothing will be able to defile yͼ
holy separtarion unto the Lord (Rom. 12:1).

Daily Bible Reading

1. Priests received special instructions on dressing a
   marriage because they were holy to God (Lev. 21:1-15).
2. Anyone with defect, even though of Aaron's desceₙ
   cannot come near the offerings made for God (Leᵥ
   21:16-23).
3. Jesus came for our sanctification (John 17: 14-23).
4. Jesus suffered in order to sanctify us (Heb. 13: 10-15).
5. God dwells only in a sanctified place and with sanctified
   people (Ex. 19: 10-20).
6. Sanctified people are to abstain from fornication and all
   things that are called sin (1 Thess. 4:1-8).

NOTES

45

THE GRACE OF GOD

Text: Act 15 1-11

Memory Verse:

"For by Grace are ye saved through faith, and that not of yourselves; it is the gift of God. Not of works lest any man should boast"
(Eph. 2:8-9).

Focus:

To learn and understand that it is impossible to accomplish any thing without the amazing grace of God.

Introduction:

Some Christians have described GRACE as an acronym for "God's Riches At Christ Expense". But it is not just at His expense, but also by His precious Blood that speaks of better things. Jesus Christ is the fullness of grace, and this Grace makes all things possible. When He shared His redemptive blood at Calvary, He made the grace of God available again to all men. Before this sacrificial act, men had no escape route from sin and the constant accusations of Satan.

Why do we need the Grace of God?

1. To ensure our salvation and to be constantly built up by the word of his grace. The Grace of our LORD Jesus Christ saves us. (Acts 10:1-4)
2. The Grace of God empowers you to do the impossible. This was manifested in the life of Paul the Apostle, from being a killer of the brethren to being a defender of their faith in Christ Jesus. (Acts 26 1-8)
3. The Grace of God is transforming. The impact of this point is felt if one recalls the personality of a fisherman.

Simon Peter was a fisherman, who openly denied Jesus but he later preached the Gospel of Jesus boldly among the learned minds of his time, availing those meant to be saved amongst them the salvation of Jesus Christ. (Acts 2:14-16)

4. The Grace of God empowers for service and good work in God's kingdom. The story of Stephen is a good example of this. The Bible says "and Stephen full of grace and Power" was performing great wonders and signs among the people. (Acts 6:8, 2 Corinthians 9:8-9)

5. It enables the believer in Christ Jesus to exhibit the fruits of the Holy Spirit. (Gal.5: 22)

Questions

Does our works determine the grace of God made available to us? Support your answer with the scripture.

Are there some people who merit the grace of God?

Prayer

God help me to appreciate your grace in my life.

Conclusion

The grace of God is unlimited. It can accomplish whatever we desire as long as is in the will of God. It is an enabler. If you do not know Jesus you cannot take full advantage of God's grace.

Daily Bible Reading

1. We are saved by grace, it has nothing to do with circumcision or not (Acts 15:1-11)

2. No more continuity in sin, but in the grace of God (Romans 6:1-4)

3. Everyone has access to this grace (Romans 5:1-3)

4. The grace of God enables us to serve God acceptably (Heb 12:22-29)

5. It is the grace of God that makes Christians willing to do the will of God (Phillip 2:13-15)

6. It is the grace of God that gives life (Rom. 5:15-17).

46

ENJOYING THE GRACE OF GOD

Text: John 1:14-17

Memory Verse:
"But to each of us was grace given according to the measure of Christ's gift"
(Eph. 4:7, NKJV)

Focus:
- To learn that we can enjoy the grace of God.
- What grace accomplishes in the life of believers.

Introduction:
Human beings were trapped and dead in their transgressions. Man can only enjoy this grace with complete faith in Jesus Christ. For it is by this grace that man is saved through Jesus Christ. It is important to note that ones' good works or deeds do not entitle one to grace, but the grace of God enables man to walk in the good works which God has prepared for him/her. The Grace of God enables us to walk in accordance with His purpose. It is a mystery of God that those that try to work for the Grace of God are ever in debt, but they that "worketh" not, but only believe get the reward of God's Grace (Romans 4:4-5).

Who can enjoy the Grace of God?

It is important to emphasize that the grace of God is available to all men, because Jesus Christ died for all men. "...to each one of us grace was given according to the measure of Christ's gift" (Eph. 4:7-11).
A beneficiary of God's Grace must be born again. He/she must be clothed with humility, because God is opposed to the proud,

and only gives Grace to the humble (1 Peter 5:5). He/she must aspire to be Christ like. Just as Jesus Christ showed unparallel humility in dying for us, washing our feet and serving us, so we must be humble. It is important to emphasize that the grace of God comes through the indwelling of the Holy Spirit, in an enthusiastically willing and humble worshipper of God. A passion for the Word of God will usher the Grace of God and the nature of Christ into a believer (2 Peter 1:2-4).

What does the Grace of God Accomplish for the Believer?
Everything, it is an enabler for every good work.
- It empowers for prayers (Hebrews 4:16).
- It enables one to endure sufferings and overcome the challenges of life (2 Cor.12:7-9)
- It enables growth in the Word and knowledge of God (2 Peter 3:18).
- It separates one from destruction (Genesis 6:5-8). If we continue to live uprightly even in a deteriorating society, the grace of God will save us.
- It ensures God's presence in any situation. God promised to go with Moses and the Israelites because Moses found grace in His sight (Gen. 33:12-17). The only guarantee to a successful endeavor in life is to remain with God. When God's grace is upon someone, such will accomplish his/her goals.

Questions
Relate personal experience where you think you enjoyed the grace of God.
How can we recognize a believer is enjoying God's grace?

Conclusion
God's grace is freely available to every believer. What you get out of this grace depends on how much you can tap into it.

Prayer
Your grace is meant to be enjoyed, give me a personal testimony in this area of my life.

Daily Bible Reading:

1. Lot maintained a righteous stand in the mist of Sodom and he enjoyed the grace that excluded him from the city's destruction. (Gen. 19:1-22)
2. Much grace is made available to those who continue to testify of Jesus' resurrection (Acts 4:32-34)
3. The grace of God does not differentiate between people. God is no respecter of persons. (Acts 11:1-8)
4. God's grace is sufficient in every situation (2 Cor. 12:7-10)
5. We are justified freely by His grace (Romans 3:23-25)
6. Those who cling to worthless idols forfeit the grace that could be theirs (Jonah 2:1-9).

47

FRUSTRATING THE GRACE OF GOD

Text: Romans 6:10

Memory Verse:
*"What shall we say then? Shall we continue in sin that grace may abound? Certainly not!"
(Romans 6:1-2a)*

Focus:
To learn not to frustrate or receive the grace of God in vain. But to use it at the time it's needed.

Introduction:
It is worth knowing and noting that the grace of God must not be received in vain according to Paul in 2 Cor. 6:1. To prove that the grace has not been received for nothing it must be demonstrated at various times and situations in our lives; such as the time we are expected to exercise patience, at the time of tribulation, needs, distress, stripes, imprisonment, tumults, labor, sleeplessness and fasting (2 Cor. 6:4-5).

Is it possible to have the grace and lose it or can the grace of God be frustrated?
Simply put the answer to this question is yes. The Holy Spirit of God who is the carrier of God's grace is gentle and does not strive. Remember Our God has said that His spirit will not strive with men. Once your habitation (your life) is no longer a house of diligent and truthful worship of our God, the Holy Spirit and the accompanying Grace of God depart. This departure cannot be stopped if you don't have the right spirit and it matters not that you are a Bishop, Pastor, usher or Sunday- Sunday Christian.

God is not a respecter of persons, and His eye sees the innermost and secret nature of man.

Signs of Frustrating the Grace of God

- The pride of the flesh (1 Peter 5:5)
- Backsliding (Heb. 10:29)
- Disinterest in the Word of God (Rom. 1:18-22)
- Failure of church going Christian to serve the LORD and evangelize in His vineyard (Jonah 1:3)
- Spiritual and physical laziness (Pro. 20:4).
- Sticking to the traditions of men frustrates the Grace of God (Gal.5:4).
- A general exhibition of the works of flesh as stated in Gal.5: 19-21.

Consequences of frustrating the Grace of God

- Spiritual Dryness and inability to pray
- Failure to abide in Christ leading to fruitlessness and withering (John 15:4-7)
- Prayers remain unanswered.

Benefits:

The benefits of the Grace of God are numerous and inexhaustible. The most important point is that the believer who operates under God's Grace is cleansed and renewed by his Word, and is constantly enabled to do all good works. The prophet Isaiah eloquently puts the benefits thus: "Then shall thy light break forth as the morning, and thine health shall spring forth speedily: before thee; the glory of the LORD shall be thy reward. Then thou shall call, and the LORD shall answer; thou shall cry, and he shall say here I am. …then shall thy light rise in obscurity and thy darkness be as the noonday:" (Isaiah 58:8-10)

Question

What is the final outcome of people who frustrate the grace of God? Support your answers with scriptural examples.

Conclusion

The Grace of God is priceless, because it cannot be earned or purchased. It is the LORD that bestows it. The Christian walk is impossible without it. The believer must come with faith in Jesus Christ and a complete willingness and humility to receive it. It is an enabler for the works of God.

Prayer

Let your grace upon my life not be in vain.

Daily Bible Reading

1. Jonah found favor in God's sight, when he repented of his disobedience in the belly of the fish (Jonah 2:1-10).
2. Joseph was successful because, he found God's grace in all his ways. (Gen 39:1-4).
3. Be strong in God's grace (2 Tim. 2:1-5)
4. Paul was counted worthy through God's grace (1 Corinthians 10:30)
5. Character matters in maintaining the grace of God (Gen. 39:7-10)
6. The Lord will not withhold anything from those who work uprightly (Ps. 84:5-12).

PERSISTENCE

Text: Matthew 15:21-28

Memory Verse:

"But we are not of those who draw back to perdition, but those who believe to the saving of the soul"
(Heb. 10:39, NKJV).

Focus

To learn from examples of people in the Bible on how to persist till we obtain desired result.

Introduction:

The Canaanite woman whose child was sick did not have a natural claim to Jesus. She was not a Jew. However, she had her mind made up as to whatever it will take to have her child healed by Jesus. She recognized that Jesus had the where withal to provide what she needed. Her mind was made up to overcome any impediments to receiving her miracle. Persistence sees opportunities in denials, hope in rejection, and possibility in every obstacle (Luke 11:5-10).

Some examples of persistence

1. **The Canaanite woman** (Matt 15:21-28)
   - ➤ Did not regard Jesus' silence as no (Matt. 15:23)
   - ➤ Refused to be distracted by the side comments of the disciples
   - ➤ Did not dwell on what was not her right, but privileges she can receive by mercy (Matt.15: 27)
   - ➤ Did not regard any unseemly comments as insults

Persistence is about getting what you set out for.

2. **The widow & The Wicked Judge** (Luke 18:1-8)

> The widow would not relent despite the wicked characteristic of the judge
> The widow would not be perturbed knowing that she was fast becoming a nuisance to the Judge.

The widow's persistence caused the wicked judge to succumb. Persistence create exceptions in an individual's case.

3. **Blind Bartimaeus (Mark 10:46-52)**
   Though he could not see, he utilized whatever he had to get what he needed. He heard Jesus was passing by, and kept shouting till he got the needed attention.

Persistence maximizes all that is available to bring into accomplishment what is desired.

As Christians we are not expected to give up at the slightest obstacle but to persevere until we get what we want. With persistence in prayer, action backing up our desire, we will get there in Jesus' name.

Questions
1. List the barriers you think existed in each of the examples above.
2. Relate how these obstacles may occur in our everyday life.
3. Propose solutions on how to overcome each barrier listed in No.1.
4. Mention common obstacles people encounter in their pursuit of excellence.

Prayer
God help me not to give up when I need to persist to achieve my end result.

Conclusion
Daily activities are not free of petty obstacles. Achievements are not made without a price to pay. Greatness is not achieved without lessons to learn. You never win a race that you quit before it is over.

Daily Bible Reading:

1. Isaac persisted, digging wells (Gen. 26: 12-25).
2. Abraham kept negotiating with God about Sodom (Gen. 18:16-33).
3. Balak did not take no for an answer from Balaam even though what he wanted was not God's will (Num. 22:1-20).
4. Zacchaeus overcame all physical obstacles to his seeing Jesus (Lk. 19:1-9)
5. The shepherd does not give up on one lost sheep (Lk. 15:1-7).
6. If you cannot let go of all, you cannot be a disciple (Lk. 14:25-33)

NOTES

49

WORSHIP

Text: Psalm 96:9

Memory Verse:

"God is Spirit, and those who worship Him must worship in spirit and truth"
(John 4:24, NKJV).

Focus:

To understand what true worship is.

Introduction:

The Lord our God is worthy to be praised and adored. Jesus clearly states that the first commandment from God is to "...love the LORD your God with all your heart, with all your soul, with all your mind, and with all your strength. This is the first commandment." Mark 12:30 NKJV. This shows that God wants the whole of our lives in worship. He wants "all of me," "all of you." One must therefore see worship as a continuous act of truthfully and spiritually surrendering one's heart, soul, mind and strength to God in totality. God wants all of me, all of my life, not a part of it. Therefore worship is what we do to maintain our relationship with God.

When does worship take place?

Although postures are good and meaningful but they do not necessarily translate to worship if one's spirit, soul and body are not all cooperating in the act of putting God in His place. It is also good to have singers stand before us on Sundays and ask us to sing praise and worship songs, but if our hearts, mind, soul or strength is missing, worship is not happening.

- When all your heart, soul, mind and strength is concentrating on God, you are worshiping. It is possible for one to have music and quietness but not worship because God looks into our hearts, not the physical things, the stimulants around us or the posture we take. (1 Samuel 16:7b).

- You are worshiping when your body is offered as a living sacrifice, holy and acceptable to God. Romans 12:1 says "...*this is your acceptable service.*" Although one is human but one's body must worship God by continuously dying to sin. Therefore each time you run from appearances of sin, you are worshiping God.

- You worship God when you put no confidence in yourself and you direct focus away from self, turning it to God in entirety and count everything but loss (Phil. 3:3-7). At this time, it does not matter who is looking at you or what your situation is; you just look into the heart of Jesus and speak to Him of His awesomeness.

- Worship takes place when one acknowledges Jesus as Lord and savior and praises are offered unto God through Him (Eph. 1:3).

- You are worshiping when you are telling your loving God how good He has been and pledging the rest of your life to Him.

What does it mean to worship God in Spirit?

You worship God in spirit when your spirit is responding to or communicating with God's Spirit. God made us in His image and breathed into us. This breath is His Spirit in us that must constantly communicate with Him. Since He has made us spiritual beings, only our spirit can respond to His Spirit. Yes, our emotions may get involved at times, but it is not enough. Truth must also take part in worship (John. 4:23).

What does it mean to worship God in truth?

When you accept God the way His WORD (your Bible) describes Him to be and you pay total obeisance to Him with no reservations in your heart, you are worshiping God in truth (Ps. 29:2). This means you do not create an image of what God should look like in your mind but you set your heart upon the "all powerful," calling Him by His names and telling him He is all that the Bible says He is, worship is taking place. At the time, a real, heartfelt and genuine communication is taking place between you and God (Ps. 95:1-7).

Different positions of worship:
There is no prescribed way or posture for worship. The only prescription is for our spirits to connect with God's Spirit in truth. Although bowing down our knees, standing up, lifting hands of praise, singing, dancing, shouting, etc. are various ways of attempting to get to the heart of God (2 Chro. 29:28). Whenever and wherever your heart puts you in reverence of God and in awe of Him, you are in good position (Heb. 12:28).

Rewards of Worship
Worship brings blessings and removes sickness (Exo. 23:25)
Worship brings deliverance from enemies (2 Kg. 17:39).

Questions
Why did you say I am not necessarily worshiping, even though I closed my eyes, singing slow motion music with my hands raised up?

Conclusion:
Our God brings deliverance. We should totally depend on Him and follow His directions. In the midst of our crisis we should always focus on Him and worship Him. We should remain steadfast in our worship and our praises. We should know that He is not only our deliverer but our everything.

Daily Bible Reading
1. God promises to instruct us on what to do, but it is our responsibility to obey Him (Ps. 32: 6-11).
2. The woman by the well thought worship was only limited to a certain place (Jn. 4:19-26).
3. Solomon worshipped at the dedication of the temple (2 Chro. 6:12-42).
4. The shepherds sought Jesus to worship Him at the announcement of His birth (Lk. 2:8-20).
5. Without a surrendered heart there is no worship (Rom.12:1-2)
6. Only God is to be worshipped (Ex. 20: 1-6)

169

50

ROWING AGAINST GOD

(Jonah: A Case Study)

Text: Jonah 1:1-17

Memory Verse

*"Where can I go from Your Spirit? Or where can I flee
from Your presence? If I ascend into heaven, You are
there; If I make my bed in hell, behold, You are there."*
(Ps. 139:7-8, NKJV)

Focus

To learn that no one can run away from God.

Introduction

Jonah was a prophet whose name meant 'dove.' (2 Kings 14:25).
Doves are usually associated with peace and purity, but could
also be a symbol of silliness (Hosea 7:11). The prophet, who
ought to know God well enough, did not want to carry out God's
instruction to go and cry against Nineveh for their wickedness.
Instead of going to Nineveh, he decided to make a quick getaway
from God's presence by sailing to Tarshish. Jonah probably
assumed that a change in location may make God reverse His
decision to send him to Nineveh. While we may be quick to
judge this prophet, a closer look at our actions in our Christian
journeys may be similar to making quick getaways as if we are
taking a fast vacation from God's presence. Like Jonah, our
runaway trips may be abruptly terminated.

The instruction was clear (Jonah 1:1-2)

There was no confusion as to what was required from the
prophet. God also gave him the reason for this particular
mission. Many at times as Christians we are fully aware of what
the word and will of God is concerning issues, but we
deliberately do contrary to what He has instructed. For instance a

regenerated person engages an unbeliever in relationship, hoping the person will become born again latter (2 Cor. 6:14-15).

Think About This: We try to make a quick getaway from the truth. What have you done as a child of God with the instructions that God has clearly given you?

He mapped out his own plan (Jonah 1:3). God has a blue print for our lives. He however gave us the right to choose. Jonah mapped out his escape plan from God's presence. Had he met with David, he would have been reminded that even if he enters the grave God will locate him there (Psalm 139:7-12).

Think About This: Take a quick stock of your life journey are you where God wants you to be? Or have you like Jonah used God's given provision to buy your way out of His presence?

He became a snare to the innocent aboard the ship (Jonah 1:4-5)

The consequences of disobedience may just not be limited to the individual offender. The poor sailors were shaken with fear. Their life was threatened, their properties they lost as they threw them out in search for solution. Chaotic and embarrassing situations may come on people just because of another's disobedience. Israelites lost battle because of Achan (Josh. 7:1-5). The whole camp had to wait for Miriam in the wilderness (Num. 12:9-15).

Think About This: Next time you want to disobey God, remember you may just bring the innocent into undue punishment.

He slept through the storm! (Jonah 1:6-12)
Chaos everywhere, yet the cause was fast asleep. The fact that someone is not yet troubled on their disobedient path does not mean one is righteous. Many Christians are 'resting' in a state of disobedience. The quiet around them is giving a false sense of security. Anyone who covers his sin shall not prosper (Proverb. 28:13).

You cannot row against God (Jonah 1:13-17)

The sailors were being nice. You have to understand limitations in life. You cannot rescue someone that God is judging. You can plead for mercy on the person's behalf. God will require repentance from the person or judgment is inevitable. No matter how much you are loved, you will answer the judgment call. Are you prepared to redirect your journey according to God's blueprint for your life? He gave Jonah a chance. He is giving you one now.

Questions

1. What are some of the present day repercussion that may come on a congregation because of the sin of a member?
2. To what extent should the church be forbearing at the obvious disobedience of a member?

Prayer

God help me to retrace my step from where I may have missed it. Let me not become a snare to others in Jesus name.

Conclusion

There is no hiding place away from God's presence. Even if you are comfortable in your sin is only for a short while and judgment will come. It is a terrible thing to fall into the hands of God.

Daily Bible Reading

1. Ephraim fled from God, sought help from Egypt (Hosea 7:11-16).
2. Achan's disobedience brought shame to Joshua and defeat to Israelites (Josh. 7:1-26).
3. Jonah prayed to God and was remembered (Jonah 2:1-10).
4. David recognized the omnipresence of God (Ps.139:1-16).
5. Saul persecuted the church until he met with God on the road to Damascus (Acts 9:1-9).
6. The angel of Lord stood on the way preventing Balaam's donkey from moving forward (Num. 22: 22-35).

Reference
Nelson's Study Bible

51

GOD OF ANOTHER CHANCE
(Jonah: A Case Study)

Text: Jonah 3:1-10

Memory Verse:
*"So the Lord spoke to the fish, and it vomited
Jonah onto dry land"
(Jonah 2:10, NKJV).*

Focus
If we return to God, He is willing to accept us.

Introduction
What manner of love has the father indeed bestowed upon us.
When we repent of our evil ways He willingly accepts us. He
restores us, and gives us another chance. This is no reason to
take His longsuffering for slackness at all.

Jonah makes a commitment to God (Jonah 2:1-3, 9-10).
Once God saw genuine repentance, He was willing to still use
Jonah to accomplish His purpose (Jonah 3: 1-2). He reversed the
punishment so that Jonah could accomplish the work of salvation
of Nineveh. When we repent we reduce the duration of our
suffering, we evoke God's mercy to work on our behalf.

Rise for the salvation of others (Jonah 3:5-9)
No one should exempt themselves when there is a call to
repentance. You may not have been directly involved in a sin but
whenever God finds any assembly wanting, let everyone cry
unto Him, peradventure He might relent and turn away His fierce
anger. Adopting a nonchalant attitude may only bring doom
upon everyone, but general prayer of intercession may open or
close the heavens. Just as we saw Ezra did in the book of Ezra

9:6-8; he lamented and fasted for the sins of his countrymen. He did not distance himself from their sins and God showed mercy.

Your works must match your profession of repentance (Jonah 3:10)
We should note that if God had meant to destroy the people of Nineveh, He would not have sent them warnings. But because He really wanted repentance, He sent warning. Therefore God saw the works of the people and he relented from doing evil to them. When we forsake our sinful ways, God will give us another chance of serving Him (2 Peter 3:9).

Questions
1. What does outward show of remorse have to do with inward surrender to God?
2. Is it in every case that people have another chance? Support your answer for or against with examples from the scriptures.

Prayer
God let me learn to follow you at initial command, not necessarily waiting for another opportunity.

Conclusion
It is not over yet. God may have just kept you to be able to hear this message and turn around to Him. All hope is not lost. Have you made a costly mistake in life, this merciful God is bringing deliverance your way today. Open your heart to Him, He is willing to show you the way of escape. He will bring you out of the trouble that might seem to have drowned you. He will give you another chance. Only let it not be too late. Accept the Lord Jesus the only acceptable sacrifice for sin. May you find rest in Him in Jesus name.

Daily Bible Reading
1. Jesus pardoned the woman caught in the act of adultery (John 8:3-11)

2. Paul invited John Mark again in ministry after initially turning him down (Acts 16:36-41, 2 Tim. 4:11)
3. Philemon was to receive Onesimus back again after his repentance (Philemon 1:1-21)
4. God forgave David for the sin of Uriah's wife, although he faced some of the consequences (2 Samuel 12:1-18)
5. God heard the prayer of Samson, and he killed more Philistines in his death (Judges 16:23-31).
6. Jesus prayed for Peter despite he knew he would deny him (Luke 22:31-34)

52

MISSION WITHOUT COMPASSION

(Jonah: A Case Study)
Text: Jonah 4:1-10

Memory Verse:
'But it displeased Jonah exceedingly, and he became angry'
(Jonah 4:1, NKJV).

Focus
To teach the necessity of having concern for others as God has done for us.

Introduction
The text of this study shows that Jonah was forgiven and given a second chance but he failed to see why God would also forgive the people of Nineveh. This is like the story of the servant in Mt. 8:23-35 who received forgiveness but failed to see the need to forgive his fellow debtor. This study will expose the selfish nature of mankind and help train us to receive the compassionate nature of God. Why would someone who was also forgiven get angry at God for not destroying Nineveh?

Mission without compassion
Jonah makes it clear why he did not want to obey God in the first place; God is merciful so He could relent His decision if the people repented (Jonah 4:1-2). He did not want a situation where he says something and it does not come to pass. He went to Nineveh not out of love for the lost souls there, but to escape God's judgment. He discharged his duties effectively, but not compassionately.

Practical Application

Many Christians, preachers, workers are carrying out laudable works in the kingdom not out of heart felt concern for the people of God, but out of compulsion. Some just to obey God, yet others for various reasons. As such the success of the mission is not of paramount concern to them as long as they are gratified. From the attitude of Jonah we learn **it is possible to be involved without being concerned**.

My word, not His will (Jonah 4:3-5)

Jonah was more concerned about his words coming to pass not the will of God being fulfilled in the lives of the people of Nineveh. His service was more centered around him than the God who sent him. It became an issue of his ego not God's supremacy and love.

Practical Application

Ministries, ministers and members alike in various organizations are beginning to loose focus of the purpose of ministry. This is generating unnecessary and unhealthy competition in the body of Christ. The race is more directed at expansions without evangelism. Emphasis has shifted from the message to the messenger. It is more about the profile of the messenger than the Holy Spirit. Such was the state of the prophet Jonah who wanted his word to come to pass at the expense of the salvation of the souls of the people.

God is concerned about the Lost souls (Jonah 4:6-11)

Jonah was angry about the plant that brought some shade to him being destroyed but God used it as an opportunity to remind Jonah that He is concerned about the people. That is why Jesus was born at all. The reason for Christmas is to remind people that there is a way out of their sins. Is not just about wishing them well and celebrating with them; it is time to remind them that Jesus came because God is still concerned about lost souls. If as a church this focus is not paramount it is time to return to God's real business- soul winning.

Questions

1. Do you think there is some element of pride in Jonah's expression about his duties? If yes how can we avoid pride in discharging our duties?
2. Why should God's will be paramount in all that we do?
3. If hitherto I have carried out my duty without concern how can I be more compassionate in discharging my duties?
4. What is the purpose of celebrating Christmas?

Prayer

God grant me a heart of compassion in all I do.
Let my focus be on your will not my personal gratification.

Conclusion

God is very much interested in repentant souls. There is rejoicing in heaven over every soul that is won. Let the purpose of the season reflect in your duties (Lk. 5:32).

Daily Bible Reading

1. Isaiah was willing to return to give Hezekiah the good news about God prolonging his life (2 Kg. 20:1-11)
2. Hezekiah welcomed the people's change of heart (2 Chro. 30:1-20).
3. Jesus forgive the woman cut in the act of adultery (John 8:1-12).
4. Barnabas accepted Paul (Saul) at his new conversion (Gal. 2:1)
5. God is not a respecter of persons (2 Chro. 19:7).
6. The good news is a message of reconciliation not condemnation (Jn. 10:10 & Jn. 3:17).

Acknowledgment:
All pictures and art works in this book
were taken from Microsoft Clip Arts.

53

TEST YOUR KNOWLEDGE

Hypocrisy in Worship

'This people draweth near unto me with their ---------, and honoureth me with their -----------, but their ------- is far from me' (Matt. 15:8).

List four types of behavior that can constitute hypocrisy in worship

1. ---
2. ---
3. ---
4. ---

Ability to quote scriptures does not represent true knowledge of Christ: explain with scriptural example.

Hypocrisy in Service

What was the name of the king that did what was right in God's sight, but not with a true heart? What is the Bible reference?
According to the book of Romans was is our reasonable service?

Hypocrisy in Relationship

Give four examples of hypocritical relationship and their outcome in the Bible

1. ---
2. ---
3. ---
4. ---

Youth and sexuality

What was the reason for various types of sexual vices in the book of Romans?

List the different types of sexual immorality you can identify from that passage.

Rebellion against God

Complete this statement "rebellion is as the sin of.............."

Where is this quoted from?

Rebellion Against Authority.

We are to be subject to all ordinances, explain.

Mocking God and His Messengers

List four traits of rebellious people.

1. --
2. --
3. --
4. --

Rebellion has consequences: Explain

Do not Envy sinners

Asaph gave some reasons why he envied sinners, can you recall some of them?

Why should we not envy sinners?

1. --
2. --
3. --

Soul-Winning: My Individual Responsibility

What is the basis of individuality in soul winning?

Give three rewards of soul winning.

1. --

2. --

3. --

Rapture

What is rapture?

List some of the events that will happen at the rapture

Why is rapture important to the Christian?

Contentment

Contentment does not mean leaving in lack explain.

What is the difference between contentment and complacency?

Sanctification
Define sanctification

Why do Christians need to be sanctified?

What do I need to do to be sanctified?

1. ---
2. ---
3. ---

The Grace of God
What is grace?

How can the grace of God be frustrated?

LESSON 9

HOW TO ACQUIRE GOD'S PEACE

Complete each of these sayings with the appropriate word:

I'm ready to throw in the … *towel*

I'm at the end of my … *rope*

I'm just a bundle of … *nerves*

My life is falling … *apart*

I'm at my wit's … *end*

I feel like resigning from the human … *race*

The Three Kinds Of Peace

1. **Spiritual**

2. **Emotional**

3. **Relational**

The 5 Keys To Acquiring God's Perfect Peace

1. **Principles**

2. **Pardon**

3. **Presence**

4. **Purpose**

5. **Peace**

ANSWER KEY FOR
LESSON 43

HOW TO RECOGNIZE GOD'S VOICE

WHY IS IT IMPORTANT TO HEAR GOD?
IT PROVES I am in God's family
IT PROTECTS from mistakes
IT PRODUCES produces personal success

PREPARING TO HEAR GOD SPEAK
CULTIVATE an open mind
The hardened soil = closed mind

3 Causes

• fear • pride • bitterness

ALLOCATE time to listen
The shallow soil = superficial mind

ELIMINATE distractions
The soil with weeds = pre-occupied mind

COOPERATE with what God says
The good soil = a willing mind

NOTES

NOTES

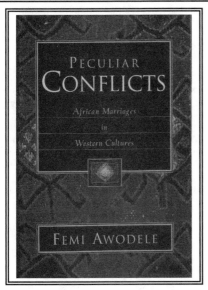
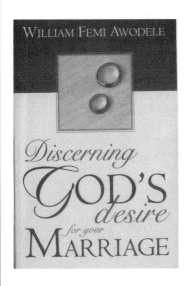

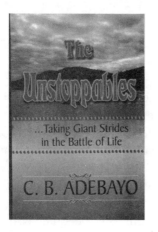

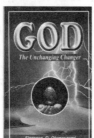

ORDER FORM
How to Order:

- From our secure website: www.christapostolicchurch.org
- By phone: (718) 658-8981 or 718-5580129
- By Fax using this **order form**: (718) 658-5317
- You could also visit us at:

108-02 Sutphin Blvd., Jamaica, NY 11435
to purchase your copy.

- Please allow 2 weeks for delivery. There is a discount of 10% when you buy 25-50 books and 15% for orders above 50 books.

Name
_____

Street Address
_____

City   State/Country   Zip/Postal Code
_____
Email

_____
Telephone   Fax

Please send order form to:

**Christ Apostolic Church of America
108-02 Sutphin Blvd.
Jamaica, NY 11435**

*$10.00 only
shipping &
handling not
included*